Mary Mercer's Dublin legacy

Maynooth Studies in Local History

SERIES EDITOR Michael Potterton

The six volumes in the MSLH series for 2024 cover a broad chronological and geographical canvas across four provinces, focusing variously on people, places, families, communities and events. It begins with an unlikely search for Vikings in the north-west of Ireland, where the evidence is more compelling than most people realize. Further south, in Carrick-on-Shannon, we trace the fortunes of the St George family from the Plantation of Leitrim through to the decades after the Famine. From Carrick we continue south to Ballymurray in Roscommon and its Quaker community (1717–1848), including their relationship with the Croftons of Mote Park. Further south still, in 1701 Jacobite Patrick Hurly of Moughna, Co. Clare, was at the centre of a 'sham robbery' of gold and jewellery worth about €500,000 in today's money. Unlike Hurly, Mary Mercer was renowned for her charitable endeavours, including the establishment of a shelter for orphaned girls in Dublin three hundred years ago in 1724. Finally, the last volume in this year's crop examines the evolution of the resilient farming community at Carbury in Co. Kildare.

* * *

Raymond Gillespie passed away after a very short illness on 8 February 2024. He had established the Maynooth Studies in Local History (MSLH) series with Irish Academic Press in 1995, from which time he served as series editor for a remarkable 27 years and 153 volumes. Taking over those editorial reins in 2021, my trepidation was tempered by the knowledge that Raymond agreed to remain as an advisor. True to his word, he continued to recommend contributors, provide peer-review, mentor first-time authors (and series editors) and give sound advice. Shoes that seemed big to fill in 2021 just got a lot bigger.

Maynooth Studies in Local History: Number 167

Mary Mercer's Dublin legacy, 1724–2024

Peter A. Daly

FOUR COURTS PRESS

Set in 11.5pt on 13.5pt Bembo by
Carrigboy Typesetting Services for
FOUR COURTS PRESS LTD
7 Malpas Street, Dublin 8, Ireland
www.fourcourtspress.ie
and in North America for
FOUR COURTS PRESS
c/o IPG, 814 N Franklin Street, Chicago, IL 60610

ISBN 978-1-80151-130-8

Printed in Ireland
by Sprint Books, Dublin

Contents

Acknowledgments

I wish to thank my fellow governors of Mercer's Hospital Foundation (MHF) for their support, particularly Richard Ensor and the late Desmond Dempsey for their excellent record-keeping and conservation. Louise Tracey continues to maintain that high standard. Kate Kelly, Director of Library Services, Royal College of Surgeons in Ireland, was most helpful as were Harriet Wheelock and Nadina Yedid at the Heritage Centre, Royal College of Physicians of Ireland. Zoë Reid, Keeper of Public Services and Collections at the National Archives of Ireland, provided access to the records of Mercer's Hospital, for which I am grateful, as I am to the staff there. Sarah Connaghan, librarian at the Royal Society of Antiquaries of Ireland, was generous with her assistance. My thanks to Anthony Edwards, Medical Illustration, St James's Hospital, for the cover photograph and to Mary Coakley for her kind support at a difficult time for her. The late William A. (Bill) Watts was chairman of Mercer's Hospital Board in 1979 when I was appointed the last consultant physician there. He remained supportive through the years and invited me to become a governor of MHF in 2002. I served under his chairmanship as well as that of the late Graham Heather and Michael Clarke and acknowledge that the board as well as their predecessors on the Mercer's Hospital board, all conscious of Mary Mercer's generosity of spirit, have worked for three centuries to see her wishes honoured. This book is dedicated to them. I am grateful to Michael Potterton, editor of the Maynooth Studies in Local History series, for his kindness and patience and to the readers who reviewed the manuscript. Finally, I thank my wife, Mary, for her loyal support in this and all my ventures through the years.

Introduction

Mercer's Hospital stands proudly at the junction of Mercer Street Lower and Stephen Street Lower with the best view of its striking cupola available from the pedestrianized South King Street. Those arriving at the St Stephen's Green Luas stop are told to alight for the Grafton Street shopping district, one of Dublin's premier retail locations. They will not encounter business concerns surviving from 1724 when Mary Mercer built her 'stone house' but, three hundred years later, in line with her desire to help the needy of Dublin, a healthcare facility still functions where that house stood. Unfortunately, it is designated in the Official Dublin Street Guide of 2013 as a 'School of Music'.[1] Mercer's has had important connections to music, not least when in 1742 it was one of three beneficiaries of the first performance of Handel's *Messiah*, but it has clearly been confused with the College of Music of the erstwhile Dublin Institute of Technology, then located on nearby Chatham Row. Today the building is owned by the Royal College of Surgeons in Ireland (RCSI), though the portion housing Mercer's Medical Centre (MMC), a primary care facility, is owned by Mercer's Hospital Foundation (MHF), a registered charity that is the legal successor to the hospital, which closed in 1983. MMC occupies the re-designed basement and the building also houses student accommodation, Millin House, and the main RCSI library, which was developed in association with the Royal College of Physicians of Ireland (RCPI).[2]

If passing shoppers were asked about Mary Mercer it is unlikely that anyone would know much about her. This would not be surprising as historians have failed to discover much detail of her life and her fame rests on the places and institutions that carry her name. Though she came from a wealthy and respectable family and many important figures served as governors of her charities, she does not appear to have had secular political influence at the highest level. It makes it all the more remarkable that this single woman, without successors, achieved so much at a time of male dominance and has left such an enduring legacy. She made full use of her contacts to the wealthy and well-positioned hierarchy of the established church and received sterling support from them and from members not so exalted. Inevitably, many worked towards making Mercer's Hospital and Mercer's School succeed but only the association with her name has survived.

She is mainly remembered in healthcare but her primary concern was the plight of young, vulnerable girls and her purpose in building her house was to provide a haven for them.[3] Dublin was prospering as the second city of the British dominions but, with a wide gap between the very rich and the impoverished, orphaned or deserted young girls were particularly open to exploitation. She saw that shelter, education and apprenticeship-training prior to entering the big bad world offered them the best security. Her 1724 initiative set off a chain of events that is still evolving. Her actions in life and the terms of her will serve as a glowing example of the mustard seed from which a plant grew and became a sturdy tree which, within its various branches, still serves the needs of the less fortunate.

1. In life

Mary was daughter of George Mercer, who was born in 1645 in West Derby near Liverpool. The Civil War was then in full flow and the decisive Battle of Naseby in Northamptonshire took place in that year, signalling the defeat of Charles I and the emerging dominance of Oliver Cromwell. Much happened as George grew to manhood including the execution of the king on 30 January 1649 and the subjugation of Ireland by Cromwell during a forty-week campaign commencing in mid-August of the same year. The Cromwellian plantation followed, through which he effected changes in Ireland more lasting than those imposed by any other figure. The Mercer family held estates in west Derby but nothing is known of their political allegiances. By 1663, when George enrolled as a pensioner or paying student at Trinity College Dublin (TCD), the monarchy had been restored with the return of Charles II on 25 May 1660. Mary's will revealed that the family had property in Ireland too. Perhaps George was avoiding some issues in England following the restoration or he may have been interested in managing some Irish property acquired during Cromwellian rule. He proved to be a bright student and became a 'scholar' in 1664, enjoying attendance without paying fees. By 1670 he was a fellow of TCD and in 1671 he was elected *Medicus* or a medical fellow. He did not take a medical qualification until 1681, however, and a year later he became a fellow of the College of Physicians. A polymath, at TCD he became a senior lecturer in Greek in 1672 and subsequently vice-provost. His career was progressing nicely before events overtook him in 1687.[1]

A rule then in force prohibited fellows from marrying and George, in an action not uncommon among his peers, breached the stricture and married Mary Barry of Finglas, Co. Dublin. Fellows's spouses were frequently presented as sisters but the truth was generally known and not challenged unless motivated by spite or the pursuit of advantage. Mercer's marriage was cruelly exposed at a commencement (graduation) ceremony of 1687 when a speech by the *Terrae Filius*, an orator designated to deliver a satirical oration in a tradition established at Oxford University, drew attention to his married status. The oration, termed a *Tripos*, was delivered by Revd John Jones, allegedly an intimate of Jonathan Swift. The most likely cleric fitting this description was John Jones BA who became a minor canon of St Patrick's Cathedral in 1693.[2] The future dean of St Patrick's has long been suspected of composing some of the content and it is possible that Swift's satiric tongue played a part in Mercer's downfall. As 'visitor' of the college, Francis Marsh, archbishop of Dublin, wrote to the provost on the matter and Mercer was deprived of his fellowship in June of that year, resulting in a major loss of prestige and income.[3] The Diocesan and Prerogative Wills Register, 1595–1858, contains two wills pertaining to George Mercer MD, for the years 1689 and 1691, and in 1702 there is a will registered to Mary Mercer, widow of Dr George. She may have been the Mary Mercer, widow, buried in St John's parish on 23 May 1700.[4] At any rate, dying as he must have between 1691 and 1702 in early middle age, he may have been affected by the tribulations that befell him some years earlier. His daughter, however, does not appear to have harboured any bitterness from the experience.

Mary Mercer was born around 1670. Though it has been recorded that she had a sister Alice, who married and had family, that remains controversial. Townsend recorded in 1860 that Alice had existed but that Mary survived her.[5] This would explain the absence of mention of her in Mary's will but does not explain the omission of bequests to any offspring she may have had unless they too had died or perhaps never existed. This matter was further confused by mention of a niece in the press when Mary died.[6] Detailing her will, it reported that the interest on £1,000 was left to her niece. In fact this bequest was to her cousin Mary, daughter of her late uncle Paul Barry, who received fond mention in the context of a gold diamond ring he had left her and which she bequeathed, along with her wearing apparel and her furniture, to Mary Barry.

Mercer lived on Great Ship Street (originally Sheep Street) in St Bride's (Brigid's) parish, just west of Dublin Castle and leading via Stephen Street Upper and Lower to the junction with Mercer Street Lower and the site she acquired. She probably worshipped at the nearby parish church of St Bride, the records of which dated from

1633.[7] It closed in 1898 and was subsequently demolished to facilitate the construction of Iveagh Buildings, a public housing project financed by Edward Guinness, first earl of Iveagh.[8] Three smaller parishes, St Bridget's, St Stephen's and St Michael de la Pole, had been merged to form St Bride's. A further rationalization occurred in 1707 when parts of St Bride's, St Peter's and St Kevin's were united to form the new parish of St Ann. What effect that had on Mercer and her religious observances we do not know but, as will be seen, she was close to leading members of St Peter's parish and approached them in 1723 regarding her building project. The old churchyard of St Stephen's parish, then owned by St Peter's, was her target. In 1698 it had been assigned to James Knight who proposed to build a house there to 'contain four rooms for poor, decayed Christians'.[9] He did not proceed and this probably made the ministers, churchwardens and parishioners even more predisposed 'to support so pious a work' as Mercer proposed. Accordingly, on 25 February 1724 she obtained a 999-year lease to 'build within twelve months from the date thereof, one house on the said plot or parcel of ground, containing four rooms, to be employed for the habitation and reception of twenty poor girls, or such other poor persons as the said Mary Mercer, her heirs or assigns, should from time to time direct and appoint to live therein'.[10]

Within a year a fine stone house, much larger than that envisaged in the agreement, was built and the work of caring for the poor girls commenced. This was the first of three major actions that would underpin her legacy to her fellow citizens. The second was the devising of her will, dated 8 August 1733.[11] This extensive and important document focused mainly on her concerns for the aforementioned girls as well as the sick and poor people of her neighbourhood. Bequests to others were something of an afterthought, reflecting a dearth of close relatives and a perception that her friends and acquaintances were possessed of sufficient worldly goods. Being a woman of pious intent, it represented a means of paving her path to Heaven, and her cousin, Mary Barry, was her sole named legatee. Her third and final act was the handing over of the handsome stone house, through an agreement of 20 May 1734, to a group wishing to establish a hospital, 'for the accommodation and use of such poor persons as may happen to labour under diseases of tedious and hazardous cure, such as the falling sickness, lunacy, leprosy and such other diseased or infirm poor persons, as the trustees named by her, and such other trustees as should from time to time be nominated and appointed'.[12] This was a completely different use to the one originally envisaged, though her will informs us that she had not lost sight of her primary goal. What actions she took to protect the interests of the poor orphaned girls during her remaining lifetime remains a mystery and she died on Tuesday 4 March 1735. As she was in her mid-to-late 60s when she made her will and concluded the agreement to hand over the house, these decisions may have been precipitated by illness and an awareness that death was beckoning.

Most likely it was her upbringing and family background that led Mercer to being so concerned for the less fortunate. It has been suggested that she was friendly with Grizell Steevens, another spinster and twin sister of Dr Richard Steevens, who, in consequence of his will, founded the hospital that carried his name. He stipulated that she was to enjoy the benefit of his property during her lifetime but after her death it was to be

> vested [...] in the right honourable Robert Rochfort esq.; lord chief baron of the court of exchequer, Revd Dr (John) Stearne, dean of St Patrick's, Dr William Griffith, Thomas Proby and Henry Aston, esqrs for erecting and endowing an hospital near Dublin, for the relief and maintenance of curable poor persons, and to be called Steevens's Hospital.[13]

He died aged 56 on 15 December 1710, just months after he had been appointed professor of Medicine at TCD and president of the RCPI. Grizell decided not to wait for her own demise to have her brother's wishes honoured and in 1717 she effected a deed appointing trustees for the planning and building of the hospital, which was formally opened on Monday 23 July 1733 with forty beds.[14] It seems a curious coincidence that Mercer devised her will just two weeks later. The language in Steevens's will and the aims of those to whom Mercer handed over her stone house seem to harmonize towards meeting the needs of those with curable and incurable conditions. There may have been more coordination than appears obvious at first sight in the planning of the two hospitals. In 1718 six French-trained surgeons established a four-bedded hospital on Cook Street and transferred to larger premises on Inn's Quay in 1728, becoming known as the Charitable Infirmary a decade later. In 1786, following a move to the former townhouse of the earl of Charlemont at 14 Jervis Street, it became Jervis Street Hospital, the name retained until Beaumont Hospital opened in 1987.[15] Philanthropy was strong in Dublin then and Misses Steevens and Mercer played prominent roles. Taking a broader view, it is noteworthy that the first of London's voluntary infirmaries, Guy's Hospital, opened in 1725. From the suppression of the monasteries (1534–41) it had taken two hundred years to begin to replace the services to the sick poor which they had formerly provided.

The situation of the poor of Dublin was already desperate by the early eighteenth century as Swift outlined in 'A modest proposal' (1729). Ireland had just passed through three years of frightful famine and, as would happen again in the 1840s, corn was still exported causing rioting to occur at the ports.[16] While Swift used irony to highlight these issues, his archbishop, William King (1660–1729), was more forthright. In 1721 he wrote of the Irish population that 'they have already given their bread, their fish, their butter, their shoes, their stockings, their beds, their furniture and their houses to pay their landlords and taxes. I cannot see how any more can be got from them, except we take away their potatoes and buttermilk, or flay them and sell their skins'.[17] Later, as the industries of Dublin were destroyed by removal of duties on commodities such as Italian silk and unrestricted importation of cheaper products from Britain and elsewhere, even those who had previously prospered such as the Huguenot weavers in the Liberties suffered ruin. The looms fell silent and pauperism replaced prosperity. In 1798 Revd James Whitelaw, vicar of St Catherine's parish, which lay between Mercer's and Dr Steevens's, undertook a census of his own and other densely populated parishes in Dublin. The data, in 500 tables, gave the first accurate account of the city and its citizens.[18] The total population, including the garrison, TCD and various hospitals, was estimated to be 182,370. Two-thirds of the citizens were of the lower class and most lived in dreadful conditions. Whitelaw recounted that

A single apartment in one of these truly dreadful habitations rates from one to two shillings per week; and to lighten the rent,

two, three and even four families, become joint tenants. I have
frequently surprised from ten to sixteen persons, of all ages and
sexes, in a room not fifteen feet square, stretched on a wad of
filthy straw, swarming with vermin, and without any covering,
save the wretched rags that constituted their wearing apparel.[19]

Between 1730 and 1800 the Irish population is estimated to have
increased from about three million to five million and, coupled
with the poor use of land and lack of industrial development,
improvements in the lot of the poor were impossible.[20] Though
descriptions of living conditions such as Whitelaw provided are not
available for the early part of the century, it can be extrapolated
from the conditions on the streets which led to the foundation of
the City Workhouse (1706) and the added Foundling Hospital (1730)
on James's Street that they were no better.[21] It was little wonder that
her poor neighbours were objects of concern for Mercer when she
made her will. Seeing such misery on a daily basis, good men and
women were moved to compassion and another manifestation was
the founding of the Royal Hospital for Incurables in 1743 to meet the
needs of the most pitiable.[22] Children born into such circumstances
were particularly vulnerable, but their special medical needs were
not recognized for another century. The first dispensary for them,
the Dublin Universal Dispensary for Children, was opened by Henry
Marsh and Charles Johnson in Schoolhouse Lane in 1822.[23] This, in
turn, became the Pitt Street Institution and the National Children's
Hospital, now a component of Tallaght University Hospital and soon
to form part of the new national service, Children's Health Ireland.

2. In death

Mercer's will ensured that she achieved even greater things after death than in life. Her remains were interred in St Mary's Chapel, Christ Church Cathedral, as she had requested.[1] The chapel, located at the north-eastern end, was converted in the nineteenth century into a grammar school, chapter-room and apartments for servants.[2] Despite her Christian charity, her memory is honoured solely in the secular domain and no church monument exists. Christ Church, though altered, still stands but St Bride's and St Peter's, where a memorial plaque might have been erected, are both gone. Her mother's will was proved in the Prerogative Court in 1702 and Mercer gained control of the family assets.[3] Letters of administration of her own will were issued on 7 May 1741, and the executors set about implementing its terms.[4] From the time she agreed to hand over the house until the establishment of the new school that carried her name at Rathcoole, Co. Dublin, her desire to serve poor orphaned girls did not have a physical expression. Indeed, there is evidence that there were difficulties with her house leading up to its transfer. Swift was then planning his hospital to serve the mentally ill and Sir William Fownes, a former lord mayor of Dublin, wrote to him on 9 September 1732 to confirm his support and to suggest where the hospital might be located. Describing the potential site, in effect where Mercer's Hospital lies, he said:

> It comes just now into my head, that there is a very proper spot, which, I think, the chapter of St Patrick let to one Lee, a bricklayer or builder. It lies back of Aungier Street East, comes out of York Street, down a place called the Dunghill, runs down to the end of King Street, facing William Street, at the north end of which some almshouses are built by Dowling and others. Also there stands to the front of the street a large stone building called an almshouse, made by Mrs Mercer, though by-the-bye, I hear she is weary of her project, and does little in supplying that

house or endowing it. Perhaps the ground may be easily come at from Lee's heirs; and by your application, I know not but that Mrs Mercer may give her house up to promote so good a work.[5]

The background to this has not been clarified but her transfer of the house and site in 1734 and the terms of her will imply that she had practical problems or misgivings. These may have related to the area and possible physical or moral hazards to the girls. Fownes's description, particularly the term 'Dunghill', certainly generates some unease. Poor sanitation was a constant problem and the presence of other almshouses was likely to attract people who may have constituted a moral risk. If approached by Swift or Fownes about locating a lunatic asylum there, that may well have reinforced her decision to hand over the property to the other consortium. In the following century the area housed many slum tenements and some houses of ill-repute.[6] There were good reasons for a move to a rural environment to enter her mind.

Her choice of executors and her trust in those who approached her to transfer her property and lease were sound. This ensured that her wishes were honoured and her legacy endured. The executors, all senior clergymen, were 'Robert, lord bishop of Killalla [*sic*], the Revd Doctor Patrick Delany, minister of St Werbrough's [*sic*] parish, and Revd Doctor William Jackson, minister of St John's parish'.[7] Robert Clayton, bishop of Killala, became an increasingly controversial character during his lifetime. His origins were also in Lancashire, near Preston, where his family owned significant estates. His father, also Robert, became minister at St Michael's in Dublin where the future bishop was born in 1695. Robert Snr was also dean of Kildare and his son inherited extensive wealth when his father died in 1728. He graduated from TCD, BA (1714), MA (1717) and DD (1730). Given their shared background, it is likely that the Mercers and Claytons were friends. Bishop Clayton lived at 80 St Stephen's Green, now part of Iveagh House, a salubrious dwelling designed by Richard Castles which was afforded high praise by Mary Pendarves (née Granville) for structure, hospitality and location when she wrote to her sister, Anne, during her first visit to Ireland in 1731–3.[8] It is intriguing to speculate that Mercer may have been a guest at functions held there during that time. Clayton transferred to the see of Cork and Ross in 1735 and to Clogher in 1745. By 1757 his controversial preaching and writings on doctrines such as the Trinity led to a prosecution for heresy. He died on 26 February 1758 before proceedings against him commenced.[9] Patrick Delany, born in Rathcrea, Vicarstown, Co. Laois, in 1685, graduated BA (1706) and MA (1709) from TCD. In 1722 he graduated BD and DD and became Archbishop King lecturer in divinity, progressing to professor of oratory and history in 1724. In 1728 he left Trinity to become successively chancellor of Christ Church, rector of Derryvullan, Enniskillen, Co. Fermanagh, chancellor of St Patrick's Cathedral in 1730, and dean of Down in 1744. A member of Swift's inner circle, he held regular weekly parties for versifiers at his home, Delville, Glasnevin. Both Delany and his second wife, the aforementioned Mary Pendarves, niece of Lord Lansdowne, left a considerable legacy of art and letters but debts rather than any earthly estate, having lived beyond their means for many years. Delany died in 1768 at Bath.[10] She was first married to Alexander Pendarves, MP for Cornwall and, on his death in 1724, moved to London where George Frederick Handel was a member of her circle. During that first visit to Ireland as guest of the Claytons she was introduced to Delany and Swift, marrying Delany in 1743 on foot of a moving and tender letter of proposal.[11] Revd Jackson was born at Maghull, Lancashire, around 1690, constituting another link to that county. A prebendary of Christ Church, he was appointed to St John's parish in 1725, moved to St Michan's in 1734 but died around the same time as Mercer.[12] He cannot, therefore, be credited with fulfilling his duties as executor, though he was still mentioned in the preamble by Hugh Boulter, archbishop of Armagh and president of the Court of Prerogative, when the will was proved in 1741.

While these eminent clergymen were the executors, Mercer placed the onward implementation of the bequests in the hands of another cohort of clerical trustees, 'the archbishop of Dublin, the bishop of Kildare, the dean of St Patrick's, the vicar of St Peter's, and Revd James King, minister of St Bride's, their successors forever or any three of them'. She would have been aware of the likely movements of such office-holders due to promotions, deaths and other circumstances. Those in office when she made her will were John Hoadley (Hoadly), Charles Cobb, Jonathan Swift and Charles Whittingham. The specific naming of King suggests that he was her close confidante and that her primary allegiance was to St Bride's. Matters became somewhat complex later when Cobb succeeded Hoadley in 1743, Hoadley having moved to Armagh in 1742 to succeed Boulter. Of note, Boulter, Hoadley, Cobb and Whittingham were all named parties to the agreement when Mercer handed over the house in 1734 for the foundation of the hospital.[13] Whittingham (St Peter's), King (St Bride's) and the ministers of the parishes of St Luke's and St Nicholas's without the Walls and their successors had further obligations as she bequeathed the interest on £2,000 to be distributed to poor, sick persons within the four parishes via visits to them by their respective ministers. Prior to death, therefore, in transferring her house and lease she facilitated the establishment of a charitable hospital and through her will she ensured that her needy neighbours and the poor orphaned girls would not be forgotten.

3. The school

Mary's will addressed the issue of the school and how it was to be funded and developed. £3,000 was assigned for the purchase of lands and tenements by her executors to be assigned to the trustees. Pending the purchase, the money was to be invested and the interest used according to her stated wish: 'for and towards the cloathing, dieting, maintaining and supporting of twenty-five poor girls and for their instruction in reading, writing and working and qualifying them to be put out apprentices and until such time as they shall be put out apprentices'.[1] If there was a surplus from the investment the number of girls in receipt of care was to be increased accordingly. The project was further supported through her devising the estates in west Derby along with properties in Dublin, in Abbey Street, Jervis Street and St Mary Street, to her executors to be conveyed to the trustees. She must have been an astute businesswoman as the will stated that she had purchased those Dublin properties. The will continued:

And whereas I have built and erected a large house and school in St Stephen's churchyard in the parish of St Peter's and city of Dublin, the ground whereon the same is built being a fee-farm lease to me and my heirs for ever and taken in lease by me from the vicar and churchwardens of the parish of St Peter's, Dublin, wherefore I devise the aforesaid house with all easements and appurtenances thereunto belonging to my said executors and their heirs upon trust, also that they may with all convenient speed after my decease convey and assure the same to the aforesaid archbishop, bishop, dean, vicar of St Peter's, Dublin, and James King and their successors as aforesaid for ever upon trust, nevertheless that to the intent and purpose that they the aforesaid trustees shall from time to time for ever settle and place therein all such poor girls as are hereby intended to be supported and provided for, and shall accommodate them therein with lodging, cloathing, diet, firing and other necessarys suitable to their state and condition until they shall be put out apprentices as aforesaid'.[2]

That clause was redundant on foot of the transfer to the hospital trustees in 1734 so there was an urgent imposition to comply with her wishes to serve the needs of the orphaned girls. The trustees must have waited impatiently for the will to be proved as happened eventually over six years after her death.

Rathcoole was the location chosen by the trustees for the school and they acquired lands in the town and its immediate environs. The extent of these lands was outlined in a map of the Lands of Rathcoole made in 1780 for the trustees and copied by William Longfield in 1827.[3] The decision was probably based on ownership of land there by the archbishop of Dublin and its long association with the deanery of St Patrick's. It was ten miles (16km) from Dublin on the road to Kilcullen, the first section of the Munster toll road.[4] It was not a Protestant stronghold but the predominant Catholic population lived in relative misery while the land and property was held by the minority. In 1732 the circumstances were described by John Loveday who noted that the road was wide and exceptionally well-constructed but that the people of the area had been inflicted with great poverty. He was surprised to see such shabby mud cabins so close to the capital city and that situation had not changed when another traveller, Thomas Campbell, reported in 1775.[5] This reflected the situation throughout Ireland and the girls at the school were relatively privileged in terms of material comforts. Whether they received much of the milk of human kindness is another question. The early actions of the governors are recorded in the 'Book of rules and orders of the Rt Revrd and Revrd the trustees appointed by the last will and testament of Mrs Mary Mercer decd'. Their first meeting, held on 4 July 1743, was attended by the archbishop, the bishop, the dean of Christchurch and King.[6] Presumably the dean was Charles Whittingham as during his tenure at St Peter's the parish was perpetually united to the archdeaconry of Dublin and associated with Christ Church. By then Swift, in his seventy-sixth year, was in decline. His female companions, Vanessa (Hester Vanhomrigh) and Stella (Esther Johnson), had died in 1723 and 1728 respectively and, a lonely and broken man, he was declared of unsound mind by a Commission of Lunacy in 1742, three years before his death on 19 October 1745.[7] He was not fit to attend and could not have been an active governor. The trustees appointed an agent, Samuel Kathrens, who had been a witness to Mercer's will. As house steward of the newly established hospital he had been found 'in every way unqualified for the office' and was discharged, only to be retained by the trustees for the collection of the rents pertaining to Miss Mercer's Charity, a position held until his death in 1772. Clement Barry Jr, described as the 'chief resident' of the village in the first half of the eighteenth century and possibly a relative of Mercer, held lands there and proved amenable. He agreed to 'accommodate the trustees with what number of acres of meadow and pasture they think necessary and sufficient at one pound ten shillings an acre, which is a lower rent than it has been set for to the inhabitants of the town, and further to shew that this demand is very reasonable, he is willing to refer the merit of his proposal to the determination of any two or three gentlemen in the neighbourhood acquainted with country businese'.[8] The trustees were pleased and considered the location most suitable with proximity to the parish church, a good water supply and a strong possibility of finding a quarry on site. Locally sourced stone would significantly reduce building costs. They had an offer from a Mr Cummin, 'a man of well-known probity and great skill in contriving buildings for conveniency, beauty, stability and cheapness', to design a plan once they made their full requirements known and to advise on how it could be honestly executed, materials selected and mistakes and impositions on the part of workmen prevented. They decided to accommodate twenty-five girls along with a master and mistress in the house and the need to teach the girls 'to milk, make butter, cheese etc., bake, wash etc. and to be thorough servants' determined the offices and outhouses required. Cummin produced the plans and John Tracy, a bricklayer, was spoken with and presumably hired. The master and mistress were John Kenny and his wife with salaries matching those at the charter schools in the kingdom. Their appointments were made while building was in progress, with Kenny overseeing the project and being paid from commencement of that oversight.

The project proceeded smoothly and the total cost was £742 6s. 4¼d. £100 was apportioned for fit-out and the first girls were

welcomed by Mrs Kenny on 29 September 1745, just prior to Swift's
death.[9] By June 1747 there was a full complement of twenty-five and
in that year a plaque was erected that stated:

> FOR THE EDUCATION OF POOR GIRLS
>
> IN THE PROTESTANT RELIGION
>
> BY THE BEQUEST
>
> OF MARY MERCER SPINSTER
>
> THIS HOSPITAL
>
> WAS ERECTED AND ENDOWED
>
> 1744

This was the first statement of a denominational requirement. No
mention was made in the will that the girls had to be Protestants or
in relation to the original establishment in the city. The decision to
affix the plaque followed a report from Mrs Kenny to the trustees,
discussed on 19 June 1747, regarding the irresponsible behaviour of
some parents. She informed King that 'many parents, particularly
of popish children, often resort to the school in order she believes to
inveigle them away, and are very abusive to her for not permitting
them to go with them to ale-houses, which she apprehends may be
attended with many inconveniences'.[10] Kathrens, the agent, was
ordered to commend her for her vigilance and to say that they desired
her in future, by order of the trustees, to discourage 'all mutual visits'.
There is no mention of anyone being expelled but only Protestant
girls were admitted thereafter. Revd King appears to have been a most
active trustee along with Dr Richard Pococke, archdeacon of Dublin
in succession to Whittingham. Pococke became bishop of Ossory in
1756 and moved to Meath in 1765, the year of his death. Though an
inveterate traveller who wrote widely on his travels, his attendance
record was good while archdeacon (1745–56).[11] Given concerns about
local ale-houses, the trustees resolved that Kathrens pursue the matter
and 'do inquire for a Protestant tenant for the White Horse Inn and
lands thereunto belonging'. Presumably, a Protestant landlord would
be more sympathetic to their views and advice. The full title of the
inn was *The White Horse and Black Lyon* and it had fourteen acres
attached.[12] Today the *Rathcoole Inn* lies on Main Street and is described
as the 'Oldest original two-storey thatched pub in Ireland, est.

1734', possibly the inn in question. The vulnerable state of the girls was highlighted in the minutes of 17 April 1747. Archbishop Cobb (perhaps fulfilling a dual role given his promotion from Kildare in 1743), Francis Corbet, a successor to Swift at St Patrick's, Pococke and King were present. King reported that Mrs Kenny was insane both in mind and in body and needed to be replaced. Furthermore, a decision was made that 'for the future no mistresses [*sic*] husband or any other man shall be suffered to reside or lye in the said schoolhouse'. This hints at advantage being taken of Mrs Kenny's infirmity and possible institutional sex abuse. Mary Owen was put in charge, with an annual salary of £12. She was succeeded in May 1757 by a widow, Susanna Harricks, who was succeeded in turn by Ann Johnston at the end of 1769. Johnston, though she received a gratuity of £12 in December 1776 for her distinguished care of the children, appears to have remained in post until November 1783, when Mary Maclean was appointed. Elizabeth Senior was in charge in 1796 and concerns about men on the premises had waned as Joseph Senior, presumably her husband, was appointed schoolmaster in March 1797. Both Joseph and Elizabeth appeared on the return to the Commission of Enquiry into National Education 1824 as master and mistress of 'the free boarding school for 50 poor Protestant female children endowed by Mrs Mary Mercer', the only school in Rathcoole under Protestant management.[13]

In 1784, about fifty years after Mercer's death, another Protestant philanthropist, Richard Morgan of Newcastle, adjacent to Rathcoole, made a similar bequest. He had boys and girls in mind and left no doubt about religious denomination. His will of 1773 sought to

> erect and furnish two separate buildings at a distance not exceeding two miles from Dublin; one to provide for the accommodation of one hundred boys, the other for the accommodation of one hundred girls, the children of poor reduced Protestant parents, to be clothed, dieted, lodged, educated and instructed in reading, writing, arithmetic and other useful and necessary qualifications for persons of their condition in life, under the inspection of proper masters and mistresses and, when of sufficient age, to be apprenticed to Protestant masters and mistresses, paying with each an apprentice fee of £5.

The inclusion of the three 'Rs' denoted that Morgan had somewhat greater ambitions for the graduates of his schools. It took many years to get his project underway with building proceeding at Castleknock between 1810 and 1813. The commissioners of the Board of Education were excited about the development and stated that in their contemporary report.[14] Morgan's legacy proved insufficient to match his ambitions and only the boys' school opened with a reduced enrolment of thirty-six.

Mercer's school remained at Rathcoole for just over eighty years, transferring to Castleknock in 1826. It had expanded to house fifty girls under the successive management described above. Rathcoole was a centre of activity during the United Irish rebellions (1798–1803) and the school could have been seen to symbolize the coercion of the majority by the minority. It escaped the attention of the rebels and came through unscathed, unlike the Protestant Charter school in Carbury at the northern end of Co. Kildare. Fortunately vacated at the time, it was attacked and burned.[15] Two prominent Rathcoole rebels, John Clinch and Felix Rourke, were executed in 1798 and 1803 respectively and the local Catholic priest from Newcastle, Fr James Harold, was deported, making it likely that feelings of bitterness and division lingered.[16] This may have been a factor in transferring Mercer's school to the vacant Morgan building in Castleknock, a decision taken in November 1823. Since the archbishop of Dublin served as a trustee for both bodies, this was probably effected with ease. On 26 October 1825 the trustees, in preparation for the move, replaced Senior with Elizabeth Williams and provided him with a pension. His wife also retired with a handsome annuity of twenty guineas. Williams's appointment was contingent on her agreement to the transfer to Castleknock where she became matron on a salary of £52 per annum with the support of a class mistress, Marianne Palmer, paid £42. By 1 June 1826 they had forty-nine girls enrolled. The Rathcoole building and benefices were let to Frederick Bourne for £25 annually.[17] The house became the residence of the local doctor but a swap was arranged in 1856 whereby the vicar moved from the glebe house adjoining the church and the doctor moved there.

The terms of Morgan's will and the decision by the trustees in December 1840 that the number of free pupils be limited to forty and that others be admitted at annual fees of £10 changed the character and purpose of Mercer's school. In time it became an integral part of the Intermediate Education System, established by an act of 1878. The Church of Ireland had been disestablished under the Irish Church Act of 1869 and questions about the denominational restrictions imposed by the trustees were increasingly asked. Such concerns were contained in the reports of the Endowed Schools (Ireland) Commission in 1856 and 1878–80. The latter report confirmed that with the amalgamation of the diocese of Kildare with the archdiocese of Dublin the number of trustees had been reduced to four. The non-attendance of the rector of St Bride's who was in dispute with his colleagues reduced it to three. Since three was the quorum for meetings it proved difficult to transact business. Notably, it was the denominational restriction, contrary he claimed to the wishes of Mary Mercer, that led Revd William George Carroll to quarrel with the others. He appeared before the Commission on 23 September 1879 and set out his position.[18] Carroll was married to Emily Shaw, an aunt of George Bernard of literary fame, and it was he who baptized the future Nobel laureate in 1856. The Shaws were not noted ecumenists but Carroll must have differed from them. It was said of him, however, that but for his temper he would have been a bishop and perhaps it was solely for the sake of argument that he disagreed with his companions.

Section 7 of the Educational Endowments (Ireland) Act 1885 provided for the exclusion from its scope of 'any endowment applicable and provided exclusively for the benefit of persons of any particular denomination, and which is under the exclusive control of persons of that denomination'. Since the Endowed Schools (Ireland) Commission provided a preliminary survey to the passage of the act, it had an important role in deciding what bodies were to be exempt. The trustees of Mercer's school were called to appear and were represented by J.J. Twigg QC. The judicial commissioners, Lord Justices Fitzgibbon and Naish, resolved that the terms of Mercer's will were such that an exclusion from the act should not be granted under the terms of Section 7 and rejected the claims of the trustees.[19] Despite this, most likely to reconcile the contrasting terms of Morgan's and Mercer's wills while ensuring the future of the joint school, Mercer's was granted an exemption. After much activity behind the scenes Fitzgibbon announced at a meeting of the Commission on 10 January 1888 that Morgan's and Mercer's school

was a remitted scheme and that 'Mercer's School has been withdrawn
from our jurisdiction', thereby denying and overturning the earlier
decision. While difficult for some such as Carroll to swallow, this was
probably in the best interests of the students and the school. Despite
all the debate and legal wrangling, however, while a new scheme of
operation was drawn up for Morgan's school and approved by the
lord lieutenant and council on 5 March 1891, the same was not done
for Mercer's and it continued to operate in line with the arbitrary
principle adopted by the trustees in 1747.

By the 1890s, some girls were doing well academically, with a
number moving on to train as teachers or to other institutions such as
Alexandra College, founded in 1866, 'to supply defects in the existing
education of women, and to afford an education more sound and solid
… and better tested, than is at present easily to be obtained by women
of the middle and upper classes in this country'.[20] Its foundress Mrs
Anne Jellicoe (née Mullin), a Quaker, had ambitious goals for young
women and like Mercer did not make denominational distinctions.

A new chapter opened in 1957 when Morgan's and Mercer's school
merged with King's Hospital, founded in 1669/70 as the Hospital and
Free School of King Charles II and first located on Queen Street.
For obvious reasons, it was also known as 'The Blue Coat school'.
Between 1783 and 1971 it was situated on Blackhall Place, today
the home of the Incorporated Law Society. It moved to its current
location in Palmerstown in 1971. A curious anomaly is that King's
Hospital, a school, retains its medical title while Mary Mercer, who
set out to found a school, is chiefly remembered for developments in
healthcare, mainly a hospital. The original plan for King's Hospital
was that it would cater for the aged and infirm poor of the city
and their children. By 1680 the governors, finding benefactions
inadequate to meet that broad purpose, resolved to receive children
only. The following report by Harris in 1766 strongly suggests that
Mercer intended her school to be modelled on what was provided for
the boys attending there but in keeping with education along the lines
of gender difference. Morgan, too, appears to have used the King's
Hospital model, which stated:

> None are admitted under three feet nine inches in height, or
> who are lame, deformed or afflicted with any infectious disease;

and those admitted are first examined by the surgeon in presence of the governors. They are dieted in the most plain, wholesome and regular manner, and are in the general extremely healthy, there being seldom above three or four in the infirmary at a time. As to their education, they are instructed in reading, writing and arithmetic; and, when they have made a sufficient progress therein, are bound apprentices.[21]

The final coalescence led to the fading of the memory of Mercer's and Morgan's schools but they are numbered among five boarding houses at King's Hospital titled Bluecoat, Mercer, Ormond, Grace and Morgan. The charity schools have moved with the times, no longer catering for the poor and underprivileged, and King's Hospital is now one of Ireland's most notable and expensive private schools. In recent years its alumni have included a president of the Gaelic Athletic Association and a Taoiseach. Such developments, even such offices, would not have been envisaged by Mary Mercer and Richard Morgan when they sat down to devise their wills. *Sic transit gloria mundi*, but none can gainsay their generosity and their legacy in education.

4. The hospital

Mercer built her stone house on consecrated ground set apart for use as a hospital leper-house many centuries earlier. By 1230 there was a chapel dedicated to St Stephen on the site, part of an extensive monastery which extended to what is now St Stephen's Green. A Memorandum Roll (17 Richard II) of 1394 recorded that Blena Mocton or Ellen Morton had lately endowed the chapel for the maintenance of such citizens of Dublin as might be smitten with leprosy. Her charity was placed under the supervision of the mayor, John Scrope, and supported with tithes from the monastery on Hoggen Green and three acres of meadow round the said chapel, and with lands at Ballenlower in Co. Dublin. Hoggen Green was the old name for College Green, once a village outside the city walls, where in 1146 a convent of Mynechins or older nuns, none admitted under age thirty, was established under the rule of St Augustine.[1] The nunnery stood on ground known as Mynechins Mantle and this was presumably a source of the tithes. Now occupied by parts of Dame Street and College Green, in earlier times the mayor and aldermen greeted the viceroy on Hoggen Green when he arrived in Ireland. Ballenlower is now Leopardstown, though it should, of course, be 'Lepers' Town' because of this association. The leper-house continued to exist until the Commonwealth but its 'Custos' Anthony Proctor, appointed in 1648, lost his title and payments then. After the Restoration in 1660 the chapel of St Stephen was merged with St Peter's and disappeared from diocesan records after 1703.[2] The site, containing the churchyard and ruined buildings, was vested in the minister and churchwardens of St Peter's, becoming the target of James Knight and later Mercer, as described earlier.

While the term 'hospital' might be applied to a lazar-house, it was simply a place to isolate affected individuals who were thereafter considered dead to the world. The ritual of throwing earth over them on entry was a visible expression of this and must have been horrific for the sufferers, making them painfully aware of the

28

sundering of their relationship with society. Neither can the term be strictly applied to the institution founded in 1724 so that credit for developing Mercer's hospital and all that followed must be given to those who approached Mercer in 1734. Her sole endowment of the hospital that bore her name was the conveyance of her stone house and the land associated with it to those trustees.[3] The complicated deed of 20 May 1734 involved four parties, Mercer herself of the first part, representatives of St Peter's parish of the second, the trustees of her previous deed of gift of 25 December 1723 of the third, and the new trustees of the fourth. The new trustees set about adapting the facility to their purposes and on 17 August, three months after the execution of the deed, the hospital opened with ten beds.[4] In operation for about six months before she died, there is no knowledge of what gratification that gave her. Despite this background, her name became firmly associated with the hospital as its foundress and that is still the perception today. Moreover, since it closed in 1983 her name has become associated with further bodies created and funded with support from the MHF.

The deed of 1734 transferred the house and site to 'John Bowes, his Majesty's solicitor-general, and Boleyn Whitney of the city of Dublin, and to the survivor of them and to the executors and administrators of such survivor for the remainder of the term of nine hundred and ninety nine years then to come and unexpired'.[5] Whitney did not gain great fame, though he was a member of the Irish parliament. Bowes became lord chancellor of Ireland and there is a monument to his memory in Christ Church.[6] They were to permit and suffer the trustees of the new hospital to govern the institution in line with the terms of the deed. The named trustees were Hugh Boulter, archbishop of Armagh, Dr John Hoadley, archbishop of Dublin, Dr Charles Cobb, bishop of Kildare and dean of Christ Church, Thomas How, lord mayor of Dublin, Charles Burton, high sheriff of Dublin, William Woodworth, also high sheriff, Revd Dr Jonathan Swift, dean of St Patrick's, Revd Charles Whittingham, archdeacon of Dublin, Revd Dr William Jackson, rector of St John's parish, Revd Dean Percival, rector of St Michan's parish, William Stevens and Francis Le Hunte, doctors of physic and Hanibal Hall, William Dobbs and John Stone, three surgeons. These fifteen, with the permission and sufferance of Bowes and Whitney, became the first governors of Mercer's hospital, with a quorum of five required to transact business.[7] It is worth recalling that Hoadley, Cobb, Swift and Whittingham were four trustees of the new charity established under the terms of Mercer's will, Revd James King of St Bride's being the fifth. In life and death she kept them busy disbursing her munificence.

Not being a corporate body, the governors were at a disadvantage in terms of receiving support such as legacies. This was corrected by the act of parliament (23, Geo. II, c. 18), already cited, to which royal assent was given on 14 April 1750. The wording of the act reinforced the impression that it was Mercer rather than her successors who founded the hospital. In fact, it was soon recognized that her stone house was not suited to purpose and in 1754, supported by a grant of £500 from the Irish parliament and some substantial legacies, the governors decided to knock and rebuild. The new building, which had improved sanitary facilities, extended westwards and was ready by December 1757. It accommodated fifty patients and capacity could be increased if funds became available.[8] The next structural development was in 1814 when an operating theatre was provided through adapting some upper wards and a purpose-built operation room and side wards opened in 1831.[9] For almost 150 years, however, the hospital's bed capacity remained unchanged until some generous donations supported expansion. These came in 1874, £2,000 from Sir Joseph and Lady Napier, parents of the hospital's honorary secretary, William Napier, and £1,000 from Edward Ledwich (1817–79), a bachelor and surgeon at Mercer's from 1861 to his death. Building did not proceed until 1887 because of the prevailing toxic atmosphere, to be described later. That development produced the elegant east front seen from South King Street. In-patient facilities remained largely unchanged from then to closure but, using £4,399 3s. 4d. derived from the Mirus Bazaar and Fête, held to benefit Mercer's at the Royal Dublin Society (RDS) in Ballsbridge, 31 May–7 June 1904, further building followed. This produced a new operating theatre, an anaesthetic room, an x-ray department and six bedrooms for nursing sisters. A pathology laboratory soon followed.[10]

The history of Mercer's hospital has been well documented in previous papers and books, particularly by Horatio Townsend, T. Percy Kirkpatrick and J.B. Lyons, and it is beyond the scope of this work to go into their level of detail. Throughout the eighteenth century the major challenge was securing funding and the imaginative methods used will be described later. Social changes which followed the Act of Union (1801) had inevitable consequences for all Irish institutions dependent on the generosity of the gentry. This class largely left for London, and serially the medical staff, voluntary funding organizations and governmental agencies took control of Mercer's.

Initially the hospital mainly provided surgical services but as developments in non-surgical care evolved that changed. It also became an important teaching hospital and, had more enlightened decisions been taken by the staff between 1785 and 1800, it could have become the leading teaching hospital in Dublin. Funding for medical teaching at TCD came then from the estate of Sir Patrick Dun (1642–1713) and a significant proportion went to Mercer's. The relationship between college and hospital was poor, however, and the Royal College of Physicians, Ireland, Act 1800 (40, Geo. III, c. 84) enabled the diversion of these funds to the building of Sir Patrick Dun's Hospital, which became the main teaching hospital for TCD when it opened in 1808.[11] The TCD medical school was in decline by the end of the eighteenth century but the appointment of James Macartney as professor of anatomy and surgery in 1813 sparked a resurgence. With John Cheyne and Abraham Colles he sowed the seeds of what became the Irish School of Medicine, which flourished for about sixty years from the time of Macartney's appointment.[12] The founding of the RCSI in 1784 and the competition it brought also served to raise standards. Leading figures in medicine and surgery included Robert Graves, William Stokes, Dominic Corrigan, Arthur Jacob, Robert Adams, John Houston, Robert Smith and William Wilde. While none of these held a position at Mercer's, medical and surgical practice was inevitably affected there and truly scientific methods became established. The founding of St Vincent's Hospital (1833), the Mercy Hospital, Cork (1857) and the Mater Misericordiae Hospital, Dublin (1861) by the Sisters of Charity and Mercy also raised standards. The medical school of the Catholic University, opened in 1855 at Cecilia Street, was the main successful component of that venture and it too contributed to improvements. Though Mercer's teaching role for TCD was downgraded, the high profile of its surgeons and their links to the RCSI meant that it became an important centre for surgical training. An important figure was the inappropriately named Richard Butcher (1819–91) who worked at Mercer's from 1851 to 1868 when he moved to Dun's. He was president of the RCSI in 1866–7 and, though only a daily average of thirty-six surgical beds were occupied at Mercer's during his tenure, student attendance at teaching clinics ranged between 120 and 130.[13] He had a significant publication record for his time. Following his departure major acrimony erupted, with surgeon Edward Stamer O'Grady cast as the villain of the piece. His surgical colleagues and their years of tenure included the aforementioned benefactor, Edward Ledwich (1861–79), John Morgan (1867–76), Benjamin F. McDowell (1869–79), Montgomery A. Ward (1879–97), and Frederick Alcock Nixon (1880–98), while Thomas Peter Mason (1865–1900), Henry Eames (1869–73), G.F. Duffey (1877–82), C.F. Knight (1882–9) and H.A. Auchinleck (1890–8) were physician colleagues. Within a stone's throw there were four private medical schools, Hayden's in Bishop Street, the Carmichael at the corner of Aungier Street and Whitefriar Place, the Dublin School at 27 Peter Street and the Ledwich, originally Kirby's, at 28 Peter Street.[14] The full title of the Ledwich was 'The Ledwich School of Anatomy, Medicine & Surgery, founded 1810, Anglesey Hospital and Ophthalmic Infirmary'. Despite having hospital and infirmary in the title, it depended heavily on clinical placements in local hospitals for student training. Ledwich had a family interest in the school and his colleagues, with the exception of O'Grady, held teaching appointments there. To the chagrin of O'Grady and others, Mercer's became a virtual annexe of the Ledwich school, something not opposed by a weak board of governors dominated by its medical members.[15] These circumstances led to a period of strife that almost caused the hospital to fail and the situation was only resolved by O'Grady's death from septic tonsillitis and bronchopneumonia on 18 October 1897 at 33 Merrion Square.[16] He was only in his sixtieth year. Earlier that year, the governors had taken the radical step of dismissing the medical and surgical staff and inviting applications for the vacated positions. O'Grady refused to accept this and the situation descended to farce with the patients under his care being denied food and he appearing with provisions for them. He continued to attend the hospital despite being ill, something which probably contributed to his demise. He was not universally seen in a bad light and a marble drinking fountain was erected to his memory on Leinster Lawn in front of the then headquarters of the RDS.[17]

As the twentieth century dawned and the dispiriting controversies ended, the governors and staff effected the necessary transformation and by the 200th anniversary of its foundation Mercer's had become a compact teaching hospital with 127 beds providing medical, surgical and gynaecological care along with a small range of sub-specialities such as anaesthetics, radiology, ophthalmology, ENT, paediatrics, dermatology and psychiatry.[18] In 1971 St James's Hospital was created from the old St Kevin's and the process of assimilating the smaller voluntary hospitals commenced. Mercer's closed in May 1983, followed by Sir Patrick Dun's, the Royal City of Dublin hospital (Baggot Street) and Dr Steevens's producing today's large modern teaching hospital at St James's.

Whatever about medical care, it is likely that Mercer, had she been alive at the end of the nineteenth century, would have taken a keen interest in nursing matters. Throughout the eighteenth and nineteenth centuries nursing care was completely sub-standard and unregulated.[19] Charles Dickens's caricature of Mrs Gamp in *Martin Chuzzlewit* was based on reality. Hospital nurses were untrained and poorly supervised by a matron, equally untrained, whose primary role was that of manager or housekeeper. The removal of untrained nurses from hospitals and domiciliary care began in England in the aftermath of the Crimean war (1854–6) and continued throughout the 1860s and 1870s.[20] The campaign to raise nursing standards peaked in Ireland during the 1880s but there were prior initiatives in the community and in the newly established hospitals of the religious sisters. Florence Nightingale, that vain and domineering woman so idolized in England and throughout the empire, was the main architect of change but ultimately she based her approach on the methods of Mothers Mary Clara Moore and Mary Francis Bridgeman and the Mercy Sisters from Bermondsey and Ireland respectively who worked for seventeen months in the Crimea caring for the sick and wounded. Earlier, during an Asiatic cholera outbreak in 1832, the care delivered in Dublin by the Sisters of Mercy from their Baggot Street base led to their being allowed to minister in some of the hospitals including Mercer's and Sir Patrick Dun's.[21] Their approach, much studied in recent years, is given the title of 'careful nursing', which is what they termed it when reporting to the British war office in 1854. The Bermondsey group led by Moore worked under Nightingale's direction but, due to the self-obsessed and volatile personality of the 'Lady with the Lamp' and religious differences, Bridgeman and her companions under terms agreed with the war office worked independently.[22] In 1852, having travelled to Rome, Kaiserwerth and Paris to observe nursing in institutions where Catholic and Lutheran sisters delivered the care, Nightingale came to Dublin and attempted, through the intercession of Henry Edward Manning (later Cardinal Manning), to spend time with the Sisters of Mercy and become a nursing sister.[23] The proposed arrangement did not proceed and that may have fostered negative feelings that lingered and surfaced in the Crimea. Her accusations of proselytizing by the sisters were particularly hurtful since there was no evidence to substantiate them, and the soldiers and civilians who benefitted from their care, and the vast majority of the army medical staff, greatly valued their services.

In Ireland, as ever, similar religious divisions arose and the development of apprenticeship nurse training and the proper supervision of nurses developed in parallel within the Catholic institutions and the Protestant voluntary hospitals. St Vincent's led the way on the Catholic front while Dr Steevens's took the initiative among the Protestant hospitals. Richard Chenevix Trench, who became archbishop of Dublin in 1864, had seen the work of Florence Nightingale and Robert Bentley Todd when he was dean of Westminster. The Nightingale School of Nursing opened at St Thomas's Hospital, London, on 9 July 1860 with fifteen probationers and Todd, a Dublin-born physician and professor attached to King's College Hospital, was mainly responsible for encouraging the Anglican community of St John the Divine to take responsibility for nursing there in 1856. Helped by his wife, Trench established a resident training institution for nurses at 152 James's Street, and the governors and medical staff of Dr Steevens's agreed to improve the standard of care at the hospital by using nurses trained there on some wards. This commenced on 1 August 1866 within a decade of the London initiatives.[24] More enlightened physicians and surgeons saw that any advances that came with the Irish School of Medicine counted for little unless nursing care developed in parallel. In medicine, clinical teaching increasingly reflected scientific knowledge and the training of nurses needed to move along similar lines. Accordingly, more sophisticated, educated ladies were recruited to the ranks of nursing, being found among the Catholic religious sisters and the socially minded, lay Anglican women of the middle and upper classes.

Over the years nurses were censured for seducing patients, drunkenness and various misdemeanours according to records at Mercer's. As late as 1874 the registrar was instructed to give in charge to the police anyone, nurse or servant, who was intoxicated while on duty or who came to work drunk. Notably, nurses were linked with servants and coming from the poorer classes they behaved like their social peers. Many viewed nursing as a specialized form of charring. A physician to Mercer's, George Frederick Duffey (1843–1903), tried during his tenure (1877–82) to improve matters. He was among the eleven members of the Committee on Nursing appointed by the Dublin Hospital Sunday Fund (DHSF) in 1878 'to inquire into the arrangements for nursing in each of the hospitals participating in the Hospital Sunday Fund'. The DHSF was a very successful charity which supported the Protestant voluntary hospitals through an annual church collection.[25] It was envisaged as an ecumenical initiative but the Catholic church, under Cardinal Cullen's influence, refused to participate. The fund delivered annual sums up to £4,000 for distribution and it carried clout. The committee's report was adopted on 22 January 1879 and Mercer's was among seven of the fourteen hospitals inspected where nursing was controlled by a person who had had no special training for their duties.[26] The maternity hospitals apart, only Sir Patrick Dun's had arrangements for nurse training in place, being linked with the Dublin Nurses Training Institution at Holles Street. What had happened to undermine arrangements at Dr Steevens's is unclear. The lack of clarity regarding the roles of ward attendants, assistant nurses and wards maids was deplored as well as the poor wages on offer to all. In light of the rationalization that happened a century later, the committee noted that much of the financial strain on the Dublin hospitals arose from there being a greater number of them than required. Among twelve recommendations it was stated that hospital authorities had a duty to provide for the efficient supervision and organization of their nurses and to participate in their training, just as was the case for medical practitioners. Supervision required the appointment of

'Lady Superintendents' as opposed to traditional matrons and every hospital was expected to arrange training by establishing their own programme or cooperating with others through a central training establishment. The implication was that funding would cease unless changes were made and it was known that the Fund ran a tight ship, as is evident in a report to the *British Medical Journal* by their joint honorary-secretary.[27] In what seemed a token response, the governors of Mercer's wrote 'that they will endeavour to carry out their suggestions, as well as the finances of the hospital will permit'. When interviewed, they had advised the committee that they could provide increased accommodation for nurses and accommodation for a lady superintendent. Unfortunately, most likely due to the controversy described earlier, they were niggardly in reacting and Duffey, the ladies committee which supported him and the DHSF, took grave exception, particularly to the failure to appoint a lady superintendent. Duffey resigned in 1882 and departed for the more compliant halls of the City of Dublin hospital while the ladies committee resigned en masse on 19 December of the same year.[28] Two governors gallantly resigned in support of their wives. In 1884, however, when matron Smyth resigned she was replaced by Mrs Canning with the title of Matron and Superintendent of Nurses. How qualified she was for this new role is not known.

The Dublin Hospitals Commission was established in 1885 by the lord lieutenant, Lord Spencer, and published its report on 4 April 1887.[29] Nursing was not its primary focus but it was a subject of enquiry during a process that sought to ascertain whether those hospitals in receipt of public funds were complying with conditions on which grants were made. It was ascertained that Mercer's employed a lady superintendent, five nurses, three attendants and two night nurses. There was general satisfaction with nursing care but O'Grady, when interviewed, referred to poor care at night in the past, though he was complimentary of a recently appointed night nurse, describing her as 'a most excellent woman of good character and with a diploma'.[30] She may have been trained at the City of Dublin Nursing Institution (CDNI), founded by but separate from the City of Dublin hospital in 1883.[31] Most of the evidence given to the commission by Mercer's personnel took the form of polemical discourses on the controversy then raging. This was extremely frustrating for the commission members and they expressed grave displeasure.

> We have said enough to show that the management of this hospital calls loudly for the most drastic reform. We do not, therefore, propose to consider in detail the voluminous evidence to which we were obliged to listen, because, in the first place, the replies which were furnished to our queries, and upon which our examination was based, had never been considered by the Board, and were often upheld in turn by one witness and contradicted by another, while in the next place the evidence as a whole presents such a melancholy picture of the relations subsisting between certain members of the medical staff, as well as the internal organization of the institution, that no good will result from making them more public than they have been made by the evidence itself. We shall, therefore, only repeat that to render this old hospital what it might be, and what from its situation it ought to be, one of the most useful of its kind in the city of Dublin, drastic reforms will be necessary, and that no reform is more urgently needed than the one which will take away from the medical staff the power to appointing to vacancies in, and of adding to, their number. This reform, it is true, cannot be effected without legislation, but the existing corporation ought not to resist it, seeing that it is very doubtful whether they have any legal existence, having regard to the manner in which the requirements of the acts under which they were created have been violated.[32]

As described earlier, the necessary reforms were eventually made and the medical staff engaged on the matter of nursing care and training. Drs Lumsden and Moore were appointed to meet with a sub-group of the House Committee to consider the reconstruction of nursing in the hospital. When they met on 9 February 1898 the case was well made, based on economic grounds and the need to raise standards. Editha Manifold, lady superintendent and matron (the terms used at the time), proceeded to recruit four staff sisters and four nurse probationers. The probationers were hired in association with the CDNI and their number increased to ten in due course.[33]

The City of Dublin hospital severed links with the institution and established in-house probationer training in 1900.[34] Mercer's continued its arrangement for probationers *pro tem* as evidenced by the furore of 1902 when relations between trainee nurses and resident medical students gave rise to grave concern and an investigation by the board. Manifold had married Richard Brews, a graduate of the RCSI, on 30 January 1900 and Gertrude Powell had succeeded her. The affair, as described by Lyons, seems to have been more in the minds of the 'narrow-minded elders' rather than a furtive encounter between the sexes. Despite this, the resignations of Powell, H. Knapp, a house-surgeon, and the dismissal of Mr Richardson, a resident student, followed.[35] Powell was succeeded by Miss Fullagar, trained at Great Ormond Street Hospital, London, and the Clinical Infirmary, Manchester. She featured in a 1904 collage of lady superintendents of the Irish Hospitals but departed in November of that year to be succeeded by Miss A. Butler who remained until 1 August 1907.[36] Her successor, Miss E.F. Beamish, stayed about a year and probably departed because of difficulties with the CDNI in 1908 relating to accommodation and support for probationers. Eleanor Hanna was lady superintendent in December 1909 when Mercer's decided to establish its own training programme. The annual report for 1910 carried the news that 'The past year was also marked by the successful inaugeration [*sic*] of a scheme for training our own nurses. The hospital is now exclusively staffed by our own probationers, and in the course of a year we will be in a position to supply trained nurses for private work'. The national census return for 1881 showed that just twenty-two beds were occupied at Mercer's.[37] Returns for 1901 and 1911 demonstrated increasing clinical activity and marked interval changes in nursing arrangements. In 1901 there were fifty-four patients and thirty-seven staff including the lady superintendent and fifteen trained nurses with just two probationers, presumably from the CDNI. By 1911 the balance had shifted and the lady superintendent now managed an assistant matron, five charge (trained) nurses and eighteen probationers aged between nineteen and twenty-seven, median twenty-three. Probationers were entered as 'nurses' and had clearly become an important component of the workforce of forty-one caring for the sixty patients counted. This remained the model of care in teaching hospitals until nursing became a degree course following the Report of the Commission of Nursing, 1998.

On 26 July 1911, at St Peter's Church, Miss Hanna married Robert Maunsell, surgeon to Mercer's (1898–1930) and later president of the RCSI (1924–6).[38] Undoubtedly, this was the hospital's stand-out doctor–nurse romance. The census of that year gave her age as thirty-one, so she could make a mature decision, unlike a young probationer. Some lack of judgment on her part or that of her husband occurred a year later when he formally complained about the state of nursing. The medical board and the board of governors refuted his allegations and expressed confidence in the matron.[39] What lay behind that is unclear but Rachael Jane Burkitt, appointed in 1912, had a long and illustrious career at the hospital and at the front during the First World War. During her absence the assistant-matron, Jenne Jordan, took charge and dealt with issues including management of the wounded from the war and the Easter Rising as well as the influenza epidemic. She received the Royal Red Cross for this.[40] Burkitt remained in post for decades, dying in 1949, aged 81.[41] Their groundwork and that of their predecessors meant that Mercer's affairs were in order when the Nurses' Registration Act was introduced in 1919 and the Nursing Council of Ireland established. Mercer's nurses wear or retain their badges with pride. They are engraved with the hospital crest depicting the Good Samaritan with the words '*Fac similiter*'. Mercer would share that vocational aspiration and admire their dedicated service.

5. Funding through oratorio, oration and odds

On 13 May 1981, as closure loomed, the governors deposited an important archive at TCD. This was the Mercer's Hospital Music Collection, assembled in the eighteenth century. It is housed at the Manuscripts and Archives Research Library at TCD and contains works performed at benefit concerts from 1736 to 1780, at least. Triona O'Hanlon has done extensive research on the archive and has recorded the contents on the Répertoire International des Sources Musicales (RISM) database.[1] She divided it into three categories, a core repertoire, *IRL-Dmh Mss* 1–44 (TCD classification), which includes vocal and instrumental manuscript sources for works by Handel, Greene, Purcell and Humfrey, those most frequently performed at the benefit concerts, a second collection, *IRL-Dmh Mss* 45–50, providing manuscript sources for Handel's Overture to Esther HWV 50 and Corelli's *Concerto Grosso* No. 8 in g minor, Op. 6, works performed less frequently at the benefits, and *IRL-Dmh Mss* 51–7, which includes seven volumes of instrumental parts for various concerti, sonatas and overtures by Avison, Barsanti, Festing, Handel and Stanley. The printed works in the third category were all published before 1743. Created for very practical reasons, the collection is a most valuable resource for scholars interested in the music of the time and how it was performed.

In 1734 the hospital got off to a relatively positive start when Dublin Corporation provided £50, soon followed by an anonymous donation of £200 via Revd William Jackson of St John's.[2] Nonetheless, they were not on a solid footing and further donations were slow to materialize. Accordingly, the governors tried various fundraising methods including musical entertainments, charity sermons and occasional participation in lotteries. The earliest records of the Board of Governors are minutes of their meeting on 28 May 1736 so the trials of the earlier years are not known. By then the practice of holding cathedral services in a city church with special music and a renowned preacher was established and the 'Musical performance' held earlier in 1736 brought in £402 18s. 2½d. General expenses were £2 6s. 7d. and there was a payment to Mr Wesley of £14 18s. 2½d.[3] This was Richard Colley Wesley, later 1st Baron Mornington (c.1690–1758), who shortly became a hospital governor. While his grandson gained greater renown as the duke of Wellington (1769–1852), Wesley was a keen amateur musician who was friendly with prominent Dublin musicians and he played a significant role in organizing these benefits.[4] He chaired a meeting on 8 August 1737 when an event was being planned and he also chaired on 20 January 1738 when the board awarded him £53 4s. 4¾d. to cover expenses. His band had to be paid but the governors also ruled that 'Richard Wesley esq. be desired to pay £10 sterling to Dr Bradford for the use of the poor of St Andrew's parish that are, or have been House Keepers'. Following his elevation to Baron Mornington on 9 July 1746, the minutes of 17 December 1748 recorded that 'Lord [*sic*] Mornington promises to continuance of musical performances but declines the direction thereof'. He was advancing in age and importance and other duties had prior claims on his time and energy.

It is surmised that Matthew Dubourg, Dublin's leading musical figure, was involved in enticing Handel to Dublin when the composer's career was not prospering in London. Dubourg (1703–67), born in London and trained by Geminiani and Corelli, became a leading violinist of his day. In 1728 he was appointed master and composer of the state music in Ireland but frequently travelled to London to perform and to meet fellow musicians. In 1748 he received a legacy in Dublin of £200 from 'a widow Barry'.[5] One might speculate that she was a maternal relative of Mercer. His friend Wesley, described as hospitable, charming and generous, was also involved in founding the Hospital for Incurables in 1744. It opened in Fleet Street, moved to Lazer's Hill or Townsend Street and was finally located in Donnybrook where it exists today as the Royal Hospital. Under Wesley's patronage, the 'Charitable Musical Society for the Hospital for Incurables' raised the necessary funds to support it through its early years.[6] His son Garret, first earl Mornington (1735–81), had a great musical talent, evident from an early age. Born just after Mercer's was established, his mother died when he was

three and, mixing with Dubourg and the other able performers of
the day, he developed his talent. By 1751, in his seventeenth year, he
was a steward at a benefit for Mercer's in St Andrew's. He remained
a committed supporter, providing services as conductor and violinist
while harnessing the support of other musicians. In 1757 he founded
the Musical Academy, which met at the Music Hall in Fishamble
Street. They gave annual concerts for the Charitable Loan Fund that
provided 'small sums, interest free, to the industrious poor of the
City of Dublin'. Mornington held sway within the academy and his
newly composed anthem 'I will give thanks unto thee, O Lord', based
on Psalms IX and XVIII, was performed in a benefit for Mercer's at
St Andrew's on 18 February 1762. He and Charles Gardiner were the
first recipients of doctorates of music at TCD on 7 July 1764, and later
that year he became the first professor of music there.[7] Much later
in 1879 another famous musician, the tenor Bartholomew (Barton)
McGuckin (1852–1913), gave a performance in aid of the hospital that
raised £200.[8] His father, Anthony, was hospital secretary/registrar
from 1875 to 1895.[9] Through these and other contacts the history
of music in Dublin was intimately interwoven with the affairs of
Mercer's during the eighteenth and nineteenth centuries. Though the
link to Handel captured the public imagination, the Wesley influence
was central to establishing the association.

The first 'Solemn Grand performance of Church Musick' was
planned for St Michan's on 31 March 1736 but was held instead at
St Andrew's on 8 April. Confusion arose and St Michan's refused
permission for what they considered an oratorio performance
rather than 'a Performance of Divine Service in the Cathedral Way',
which was intended.[10] Many parishes were not content to host
benefit performances but those modelled on the services of worship
held in London by the 'Corporation of the Sons of the Clergy'
were generally accepted. The first of these was held at old St Paul's
Cathedral on 8 November 1655 and, subsequently, leading musicians
were generous with their support in London and Dublin. Handel's
music was particularly popular, though also controversial at the time,
and his *Te Deum and Jubilate*, which celebrated the Treaty of Utrecht
(1713) and a coronation anthem written for the accession of George
II in 1727 constituted the music for the service on 8 April 1736. The
preacher was Revd John Madden, dean of Kilmore and vicar of St

Ann's. The menu varied little and was repeated at St Andrew's on 13 February 1738 with a sermon by the bishop of Kildare, Charles Cobb, and on 16 February 1740 with the bishop of Ferns as preacher. Until 1780, at least, benefits for Mercer's were held annually or bi-annually, usually in February or December, becoming major events in the social calendar. The concerts were attended by leading members of the aristocracy and government officials up to the viceroy. The duke of Dorset, who occupied that position in 1736, set a trend by attending the first benefit.[11] A bond was cemented between the institution and prominent citizens and, though generation of funds was the primary objective, those feelings of affection were critical to the hospital's survival.

While the motives and generosity of such as Mercer and Grizell Steevens can hardly be questioned, those of others may not have been so pure, philanthropic or disinterested. Writing about the proposal to build a hospital for incurables, Swift commented that 'there was nothing that redounded more to individual reputations or national honour than the establishment of and support of institutions for the relief of different types of distress. The diseased and unfortunate are thereby delivered from the misery of wanting assistance, and others are delivered from the misery of beholding them'.[12] His views were confirmed by a report in Watson's Almanack for 1750 regarding the Hospital for Incurables.

> Since the opening 111 miserable creatures have been admitted. 28 are now in the house. They are maintained, furnished with cloaths, linen and other necessaries and when they die are decently buried ... the wretched are here maintained, their infirmities palliated, and the publick in a great measure freed from those disagreeable sights so frequently heretofore met with in our streets.[13]

The church services and charity sermons, as major social occasions, were planned long in advance and attendance was maximized through avoiding clashes with other events. Procuring a noted preacher was critical and neighbouring churches usually closed so that alternative venues for worship were unavailable. Men of rank, acting as stewards, kept order and ladies of status and beauty served as collectors. In later years the music was dropped and a divine service preceded the sermon. Attention during service was often poor but the preacher had the undivided ear of the congregation once he ascended the pulpit. Having aroused feelings of guilt and benevolence he signalled the collection, which took place to a carefully designed strategy. A silver salver was passed around but, regularly tipped into a container; it was presented empty to each pew.[14] 'Thus every engine is moved to increase the collection; and the charity of the congregation is so far from being the simple dictate of religion, that it is a mixed emotion, in which eloquence, pity, beauty and vanity have a considerable share'.[15] Aspects of the process changed following the Act of Union as demonstrated in a letter from J. Digges Latouche, a governor of Mercer's, to Sir William Gosset, under-secretary of state, on 8 November 1831. Gosset was requested to be a collector so it appears the ladies were no longer performing that role.[16] An epidemic of cholera in Dublin at the time, however, may have led to unusual arrangements. The preacher was Revd Robert Daly, the leading evangelical clergyman of the time, rector of Powerscourt and later bishop of the united dioceses of Cashel, Emly, Waterford and Lismore.[17]

Handel arrived from Chester on 15 November 1741 and took an interest in supporting the newly founded hospital. He was well-disposed to the Irish aristocracy and the projects they supported having enjoyed the patronage of Richard Boyle, third earl of Burlington and fourth earl of Cork, in London and, invited to Dublin by the viceroy, William Cavendish, third duke of Devonshire, was given assurances of support.[18] The duke regularly supported Mercer's and its fundraising functions. Handel's music would have been well known to Mercer but alas she was not there to meet or thank him. The annual benefit performance had been arranged for 10 December at St Andrew's and Handel was invited to play the organ.[19] The programme again consisted of his *Te Deum and Jubilate* and two of his anthems. William Boyce (1710–79) somewhat upstaged him, however, having composed a grand anthem for the occasion. Handel attended but it is not known if he played the organ. He was promptly thanked for his attendance while Boyce was not formally thanked until early January.[20] Some controversy arose in that Handel's attendance somewhat overshadowed Boyce's anthem and others, the earl of

Shaftsbury included, felt it was an insult to Handel to ask him to play in accompaniment to the work.[21] Boyce was perceived as a disciple of Maurice Greene, a great London rival to Handel and this added spice. Boyce's anthem, 'Blessed is he that considereth the sick and needy', was repeated to benefit Mercer's on 12 December 1745 at St Michan's but then virtually disappeared until a performance, directed by Marion Doherty Hayden, was given at the RCPI on 14 November 1990 to mark the founding of Mercer's Institute for Research on Ageing (MIRA).[22]

The opening of the 'Great Music-Hall', also known as Neale's Music Hall, on Fishamble Street just weeks before his arrival was a boon to Handel.[23] In late 1741 and early 1742 he arranged two series of six concerts there and, contrary to his recent experience in London, they were a resounding success.[24] The first series concluded with a concert on 10 February and the second on 7 April. Arrangements proceeded for the premiere of 'Messiah' and, demonstrating Handel's assiduity, a full rehearsal was held on 8 April, with the first performance scheduled for the Music Hall on 13 April. Purchasers of tickets, at half a guinea each, were entitled to a free ticket for the rehearsal.[25] Rarely mentioned in the context of 'Messiah' is Charles Jennens of Gospall Hall in Leicestershire who selected the scripture passages so movingly set to music. The two men remained close friends until Handel died in 1759 and he frequently referred to 'your Messiah' when writing to Jennens.[26]

The hall was filled for the rehearsal and, to ensure that maximum room was available, ladies were requested to 'come without hoops'. That request was repeated for the main performance and gentlemen were 'desired to come without their swords', ensuring that an audience of seven hundred was accommodated.[27] Dubourg led the band and members of the choirs of St Patrick's and Christ Church combined in a special chorus. The participation of members of the cathedral choirs was not easy to arrange, given the secular venue and the nature of the performance, but was facilitated by John Wynne, precentor of St Patrick's, acting as sub-dean in face of Swift's infirmity. Wynne, also a governor of Mercer's, had been treasurer in 1740 and was acutely aware of financial needs. No doubt he exercised his influence at St Patrick's and liaised with his counterpart at Christ Church, Revd Gabriel James Maturin, to facilitate arrangements.[28] Ironically for

Wynne, Maturin was appointed to succeed Swift in 1745. Male solo parts were assigned to choir members and the female soloists were Christina Maria Avoglio, soprano, and Susannah Cibber, contralto. A rave review was published on the following Saturday.

> On Tuesday last, Mr Handel's Sacred Grand Oratorio, the Messiah, was performed in the new music hall in Fishamble Street; the best judges allow it to be the most finished piece of musick. Words are wanting to express the exquisite delight it afforded to the admiring crowded audience. The sublime, the grand, and the tender, adapted to the most elevated, majestic and moving words, conspired to transport and charm the ravished heart and ear. It is but justice to Mr Handel that the world should know he generously gave the money arising from this grand performance to be equally shared by the Society for relieving Prisoners, the Charitable Infirmary, and Mercer's Hospital, for which they will ever gratefully remember his name: and that the gentlemen of the two choirs, Mr Dubourg, Mrs Avolio and Mrs Cibber, who all performed their parts to admiration, acted also on the same disinterested principle, satisfied with the deserved applause of the publick, and the conscious pleasure of promoting such useful and extensive charity. There were above 700 people in the room, and the sum collected for that noble and pious charity amounted to about £400, out of which £127 goes to each of the three great and pious charities.[29]

Prisoners of the Marshalseas were probably the most immediate beneficiaries and the Charitable Musical Society, many of whose members played, reported later that 142 prisoners were released on discharge of debts amounting to £1225 17s. 1d. during 1742.[30]

Numerous other favourable press commentaries appeared including a poem of praise and it was no surprise that Handel cashed in on this. He presented a performance of 'Saul' on 25 May and a repeat performance of 'Messiah' on 3 June, tickets at half a guinea for both. Considering the capacity of the hall, income must have been close to one thousand guineas but he and his colleagues deserved such reward given their earlier charity. These were his final Irish performances and he left on 13 August but never revisited what he termed 'that generous and polite nation'.[31] His music featured prominently in benefit concerts during the following decades and, much later in 1859 Jenny Lind, the Swedish nightingale, gave an oratorio performance in Dublin to mark the centenary of his death. The beneficiaries were Mercer's and the Charitable Musical Society for the Relief of Distressed Musicians, two Irish charities added to numerous others that Lind supported in her native Sweden and the US. She visited the hospital and must have recognized a kindred spirit in Mercer. An address was read and presented to her by Horatio Townsend, then a governor and historian of the early days of the hospital and author of an account of Handel's Dublin sojourn.[32]

With over twenty musical benefits, doubled in number by rehearsals, held up to 1771 the practice ran out of steam and from 1780 onwards they were replaced by charity sermons. These took place on a similar schedule at St Ann's and St Peter's exclusively, always on Sundays, until 1833. In 1874 the DHSF was founded to provide support to the voluntary hospitals. During the first one hundred years, therefore, Mercer's derived support from musical events and charity sermons. As an income stream they were exceeded by personal benefactions, legacies and rental receipts. Minutes of 26 October 1751 showed annual subscriptions delivering £144 14s. 3d., benefactions and legacies £247 13s. 10½d. and the 'Benefit by last year's musick', £161 15s. 3½d. Effective in raising income, the musical events were copied by other Dublin hospitals. These performances placed Mercer's, along with the two cathedrals, to the forefront in bringing such works to the people and the highly significant Mercer's music archive was created.

The lottery method of generating support did not prove durable and, following an initial foray in January 1741 when a lottery delivered £805 5s. 6½d. each to the Charitable Infirmary, Dr Steevens's and Mercer's, participation became intermittent and was eventually abandoned.[33] The 1741 sum was significant but the effort probably too uncertain and exhausting. Such revenue was considered by many to be tainted and lotteries morally suspect. The Rotunda opened in 1765 and there and in public rooms beside the lying-in hospital up to £1,000 per year was raised through gambling. Pressure from the 'Association for Discountenancing Vice' caused the governors of the Rotunda to abandon this practice. As an alternative, from 1785 they became entitled to the proceeds of a levy on sedan chairs, but that market declined following the Act of Union.[34] Money from the Irish Hospitals' Sweepstake, raised between 1930 and 1987, supported Mercer's as part of the Irish hospital system, though the governors did not immediately embrace support from that quarter.

As time passed the state became increasingly involved in healthcare delivery. The first official recognition of the role of the charitable infirmaries was the Act for Erecting and Establishing Publick Infirmaries or Hospitals in the Kingdom (5 Geo. III, c. 20, s. 13) passed by the Irish parliament in 1765. It stated 'and whereas 3 publick infirmaries or hospitals have been erected in the city of Dublin, one called the Charitable Infirmary on Inn's Quay, another Mercer's Hospital in St Stephen's Street and third, the Hospital for Incurables on Lazer's Hill and are supported by voluntary subscriptions which are not sufficient for providing physicians or surgeons and food, medicines and other necessaries for the poor patients therein, therefore be it enacted that the yearly sum of £150 shall be paid out of publick money to the Treasurer of the Charitable Infirmary, Mercer's Hospital and the Hospital for Incurables, to be equally divided between them'. Though not a large sum, it established the principle of state support. Dr Steevens's was omitted, presumably having better income from the original bequest and its many benefactors. Among those who bestowed a founding legacy was Esther Johnson or Swift's 'Stella', in 1723.[35] This represented restricted funding as it was for the maintenance of the chaplain to Dr Steevens's, which had its own chapel up to modern times. Payments to consultants at all voluntary hospitals remained low up to 1981 when the common contract was introduced. Up to that, initially gratis and then for little recompense with no pension or other benefits, they provided care to public patients. The closure of Mercer's, following hard on the introduction of the common contract, was greatly facilitated by the availability of pensions for those at or beyond retirement age. The days when hospital care could be provided without charge and fundraising, with minimal government support, could support day-to-day activity were long past.

6. The street and buildings

Upper Mercer Street was originally called French Street and the Lower portion was Love Lane. The latter, according to Sir William Fownes's letter to Swift in 1732, must have been known earlier as the Dunghill.[1] Even with its less-malodorous title it acquired a bad reputation, presumably from what was transacted in the guise of love, and it was renamed in 1773.[2] When the RCSI built their new facility about fifteen years later it appeared on plans as 'formerly Love Lane, now Mercer Street'.[3] In 1806 the Carmelite priests, or Whitefriars, moved from Ash Street in the Liberties to French Street and built a chapel in Cuffe Lane. In 1825 they rebuilt at the location of their original monastery of 1278, dissolved in 1539, and what was Whitefriars' Lane became Whitefriar Street. The Order provided a chaplaincy service to Catholic patients at Mercer's from then to its closure. It was 1860 before French Street was renamed.[4] As with Whitefriar Street, the presence of the hospital and the acknowledgment of its original benefactress in its title suggested an obvious new designation for it and Love Lane. Mercer Street Upper runs between Cuffe and York streets and Mercer Street Lower runs between York and Stephen Street Lower with the hospital on the western side at the northern end. The area underwent a radical decline during the nineteenth century when many of the houses became tenements with the associated problems of poverty and overcrowding. Thom's Irish Almanac 1862 showed thirty-eight tenements on the upper portion and just five businesses in operation: two grocers, a shoemaker, a carpenter/builder and a solicitor. Mercer Street Lower retained a greater semblance of a city street with at least ten businesses operating in addition to the hospital. It had nine tenements and three vacant properties, however, indicating that it too was in decline.

The RCSI received a royal charter from George III on 11 February 1784 and, having failed to obtain financial support from parliament to build, they leased a building on Mercer Street, previously used to house the charity children of St Peter's parish. To gain access to Goat Alley, now Digges Lane, they bought an adjoining house, important for getting bodies discreetly, indeed surreptitiously, brought in for dissection. From its inception, the RCSI was closest to Mercer's and four of the surgeons who petitioned for the charter held appointments there, further consolidating links. They were George Daunt, Gustavus Hume, Francis Foreside and Henry Morris.[5] In time, fourteen surgeons with appointments to Mercer's became presidents of the college.[6] The RCSI remained in Mercer Street from 1789 to 1810 when it moved to buildings erected on an old Quaker burial site in St Stephen's Green. The original buildings on Mercer Street generated significant disagreement with the hospital governors and, though legal opinion was sought regarding encroachment by the college on hospital property, legal action was avoided and the matter settled amicably. The two-storey building that housed the 'Schools of Surgery on Mercer Street' had a dissecting room and offices on the ground floor with a theatre, museum of anatomical specimens and a preparation room on the floor above. The hospital, then sixty years in existence, appeared on the RCSI plans as a simple rectangular block with limited frontage to Stephen's Street and Johnston Place. The governors had understandable concerns about being hemmed in by any adjoining developments. It must have been a relief, therefore, to have had the option of acquiring the college premises. The RCSI committee overseeing the transfer and disposal of the old buildings recommended in May 1809 that the hospital should be offered a piece of ground between Goat Alley and their premises held by them at a yearly rent of £3 10s., having purchased it for a hundred guineas. They also proposed surrendering a building beside that, lying at the rear of the hospital, with a number of conditions attached; the hospital would pay the yearly rent of £3 10s. and would share the expense of constructing a boundary wall. The governors replied expressing the hope that the college would show support for their charitable institution by donating the old college on the terms by which they held it. Battle lines were redrawn with lawyers for both sides involved but in February 1811 the renowned surgeon Abraham Colles announced a resolution. The college premises were to be sold to the hospital for £300 but with conditions attached. The lawyers agreed, in their usual dense language, that the deed of the premises to which the college can show a good title be executed forthwith in consideration of £200. The remaining one hundred of the purchase money to be at the same time paid down to the college on their receipt for it; and promising therein to execute a deed for the other premises when tendered to them for that purpose by the hospital.[7]

Apparently the RCSI could produce deeds of title for some of the property conveyed to them by Patrick Byrne in 1789. He, in turn, held his title from the minister and church wardens of St Peter's parish, as did the hospital. Simply stated, the hospital was to pay £200 with the balance due once title to the disputed area was resolved. It is unclear if that final payment was ever made. Regardless, Mercer's now had extensive frontage to Mercer Street Lower, which greatly facilitated development in the succeeding years and rear access was also enhanced. Financial constraints described earlier, however, meant that the opportunity to expand could not be availed of for many years.[8]

In Ireland, the Industrial Revolution occurred mainly in the north-east with Belfast at its centre, leaving Dublin largely unaffected. Rural poverty, nonetheless, drove large numbers to the capital where they lived in a state of squalor unparalleled in Britain. Sir Charles Cameron, medical superintendent and executive officer of health, public analyst and inspector of explosives, gave the following description.

In 1903 the registered tenement houses numbered 6,195, and in them more than a third of the population of Dublin resided. Above one-third of these houses had at one time or another been de-tenanted and closed as unfit for human occupation, but had been repaired and re-opened. About 1,000 similar houses which had been closed are now in ruins or have completely vanished, leaving only their sites. All through the city these ruins and vacant sites can be seen. At the present moment there are at least 20,000 persons whose dwellings urgently require to be radically improved.[9]

The situation was worse when Ireland gained independence in 1922 and the problem had to be addressed by the fledgling government in the face of almost crippling economic adversity. Great progress was made during those early years. Among the deprived areas redeveloped was Mercer Street where construction of public housing was under the initial guidance of Horace Tennyson O'Rourke (1880–1963), Dublin city architect 1922–45,[10] and later Herbert George Simms (1898–1948). While O'Rourke was a native Dubliner, Simms was a Londoner who fought with the Royal Field Artillery in the First World War and then studied architecture in Liverpool on an ex-service scholarship.[11] From 1924, with the exception of a short period in India in 1929, Simms held various positions with Dublin Corporation. When Fianna Fáil came to power in 1932 they established a separate architectural department to address the housing problem with Simms in charge. The efforts of the two men produced three detached blocks of multiple-bay, three-storey-with-attic social-housing apartments on upper Mercer Street. They are set back from the street, with landscaped front areas, enclosed by iron railings set on concrete plinths with matching gates hung on brick piers that provide access to the rear. The original design was O'Rourke's and the first phase was built between 1926 and 1930; the second phase was completed by Simms between 1932 and 1934 using O'Rourke's design. Simms's later title was Dublin City's Housing Architect. The blocks, two on the east side and one on the west, retained much of the original character and materials of the area and their overall form, mansard roofs and contrasting brickwork were derived from the arts-and-crafts tradition in line with the latest trends in flat development in English cities.[12] They have stood the test of time well and they afforded people the opportunity to remain in their inner-city habitat rather than being forced to move to new suburban estates. The social consequences of such an upheaval have been described by many Dublin writers including Brendan Behan and his mother.[13] The apartments comprise two bedrooms, bathroom, kitchen and living-room and have gas-fired central heating, making them very desirable to those needing public housing.

Fired with a sense of new-found freedom and to commemorate those who had delivered it, such housing developments were frequently named after revolutionaries, among them Constance Markiewicz and Madeleine ffrench-Mullen. It was a tribute to Mercer and the care provided to the community by the hospital that

the new blocks were named Mercer House. No such tribute was paid
to Simms who died of horrific injuries when hit by a train while of
unbalanced mind on 28 September 1948.[14] Pressure of work, no doubt
exacerbated by the legacy of his war experiences, led him to take
his own life, aged 50. O'Rourke had a happier outcome, dying at 83
from natural causes. One can still see their legacies on Mercer Street
and elsewhere in Dublin but, along with Cameron and others, they
remain unsung heroes despite delivering vastly improved housing and
sanitary conditions to the city.

7. Mercer's Hospital Foundation

When, in its bi-centenary year of 1984, the RCSI purchased Mercer's it represented a neat rounding of a circle. Initially there was talk of demolishing the building, but this was strenuously opposed by many, including An Taisce. Ultimately, behind the elegant façade, a very sympathetic renovation was done under the stewardship of a committee chaired by J. Dermot O'Flynn. A later committee, the 'RCSI New Horizons in Medical Education II, Mercer's Development Fund', chaired by Francis A. Duff had four aims; to develop a community healthcare centre to serve the college and local communities and house the newly founded department of family practice, to develop a modern medical library, to increase laboratory and research space and to expand residential accommodation and social amenities for students. The old nurses' home was particularly suited to the last purpose and became Millin House. The redevelopment was completed in a timely manner and officially opened by President Mary Robinson on 9 April 1991.[1]

Anyone familiar with the Irish healthcare service during the 1980s will remember the restrictions and cutbacks necessitated by a growing economic crisis. The closure of Mercer's in 1983 took place in a well-planned, structured manner but, as the recession deepened and cuts to expenditure became greater, the push to close the other designated hospitals became more urgent. Closure was no longer focused on rationalizing and improving services but rather on efficiencies and cost reductions. Accordingly, the transfer of services from Sir Patrick Dun's to St James's occurred more hastily in August 1987. In a fateful move, obstetrical services were closed at St James's and transferred to the Coombe Hospital in September of that year, creating space for the hurried transfer of services from Baggot Street and Dr Steevens's. The Department of Health (DOH), heady no doubt from the feeling of power that flowed from such perceived success, declared an expectation that the £850,000 from the sale of Mercer's should enter their coffers. That view was not shared by the board of governors who considered the funds theirs as long as they were applied to the aims of the founders. In July 1982, prior to closure, the medical board of Mercer's considered how the money might be used and resolved that it should take the form of bricks and mortar through the establishment of a centre for the care and rehabilitation of the elderly at St James's. This was communicated to the governors and to the St James's/Federated Voluntary Hospitals (FDVH) joint medical committee, which further resolved on 13 December 1982 that the name of Mary Mercer should be perpetuated within the St James's campus following the closure of Mercer's and that a centre for the care and rehabilitation of elderly patients on the St James's site should be established. The first aspiration was fulfilled in 1995 when a thirty-one-bed ward in the new hospital was named Mary Mercer's ward, designated for care of the elderly, but building a specialized centre was a more difficult task. Responding to the DOH demand for the money, the chairman, TCD provost William Arthur Watts, used the rather frivolous analogy of the motorist who purchased fuel consistently at a garage for many years not expecting to own it if it were sold.[2]

After much discussion and legal opinion, the matter came before Miss Justice Mella Carroll of the High Court (1986 No. 975 Sp.) for decision on 16 March 1987. Her judgment created the Mercer's Hospital Foundation (MHF) under an approved cy-près scheme, 'a legal doctrine which allows a court to amend a legal document to enforce it "as near as possible" to the original intent of the instrument, in situations where it becomes impossible, impracticable or illegal to enforce it under its original terms'. The legal documents requiring amendment were the indenture dated 20 May 1734 and the act, Geo. II, 25 March 1750, referred to in earlier chapters. To inform the court, affidavits were sworn and filed on 28 October 1986 by Watts, chairman of Mercer's board, Desmond J. Dempsey, CEO of the FDVH and Kieran Hickey, programme manager of the Eastern Health Board (EHB), the relevant agency of the DOH. Watts's affidavit was seventeen pages long and, over thirty-four paragraphs he outlined the history of the hospital, the decisions surrounding closure and transfer of services, the financial details, and possible plans for the future.[3] He appended three short histories of Mercer's that had been published in medical journals and 'The Mercer's Foundation – a

Table 1. Governors of Mercer's Hospital Foundation

Name	Term	Chair	Vice-chair
W.A. Watts	1987–2010 (d.)	1987–2003	
J.W. Brooks	1987–1997 (d.)		
M.H.M. Clarke	1987–present	2017–2023	2004–2017
A.F. Grey	1987–2016 (d.)		
R.G. Hall	1987–1991 (rtd)		
R.G. Heather	1987–2017 (d.)	2003–2017	1997–2003
J.W.P. Hoblyn	1987–1998 (rtd)		
J.G. Mathews	1987–1998 (d.)		
D. Robinson	1987–2010 (d.)		
J.E. Coolican	1994–2004 (rtd)		
D.J. Dempsey	1997–2006 (rtd)		
F.C. Winkelmann	2000–2007 (rtd)		
P.A. Daly	2002–present	2023–present	2018–2023
R.S.G. Ensor	2005–present		2023–present
A.S. Doak	2005–2014 (rtd)		
C. Geelan	2005–2018 (rtd)		
G. Wilson	2005–present		
P. Hayes	2011–present		
C. Heather	2012–2023 (rtd)		
M. Costello	2016–present		
P. Robinson	2016–present		
Grania Clarke	2022–present		
J. Hudson	2022–present		

proposal', a detailed document prepared by Davis Coakley and Jim Malone regarding the establishment of a centre of excellence for care of the elderly at St James's. He informed the court that £801,858 of the sale price remained which, pending the outcome of the hearing, was on deposit with the Agricultural Credit Corporation, a bank owned by the Irish government. Hickey's affidavit consisted of four pages (seven paragraphs) supporting the Coakley/Malone proposal, which already had the support in principle of the Mercer's and St James's boards. Dempsey's sworn statement described the relationship between Mercer's and the FDVH, confirming that the central council of the FDVH had never exercised any statutory powers conferred by sections 16 and 17 of the 'said act' in respect of Mercer's. The FDVH was founded under the terms of the 'Hospitals Federation and Amalgamation Act', which became law on 8 July 1961.[4] The seven institutions covered, all voluntary teaching hospitals associated with TCD, were the Adelaide (1839), Dr Steevens's (1733), the Meath Hospital and County Infirmary (1753), Mercer's (1734), the Royal City of Dublin, Baggot Street (1832), Sir Patrick Dun's (1808) and the National Children's Hospital (1821). C.F. Dowling, a civil servant, became the first secretary to the Central Council of the FDVH but it was later managed by a CEO, the first being Nevin Dowling with Dempsey being his immediate successor.[5] It was important to demonstrate that Mercer's had functioned autonomously up to its closure and could, therefore, act independently in legal matters. The governors of Mercer's were plaintiffs and the Attorney General was defendant in the case. In awarding costs to both parties, payable 'out of the property of the said charity', Miss Justice Carroll did transfer a modicum of the sale price to the state but the majority remained with the governors to be invested and used in accordance with the cy-près scheme. At the end of November 1985 the value was £929,890, reflecting high interest rates on deposits at the time.[6]

The scheme was approved by the Commissioners of Charitable Donations and Bequests (CCDB) on 28 July 1987. The MHF was immediately constituted and met under the chairmanship of Watts. The eight other appointees had also been hospital governors at closure; J.W. Brooks, M.H.M. Clarke, A.F. Grey, R.G. Hall, R.G. Heather, J.W.P. Hoblyn, J.G. Mathews and D.F. Robinson (table 1). Desmond Dempsey was appointed secretary to the new board.[7] The governors had £1,219,425 at their disposal from the investment and faced a new challenge; rather than governing the running of a hospital, they had to focus on fulfilling the wishes of the founders within the terms of the scheme and guided by the stated objects of the foundation. The defined objects in the judgment of the High Court were:

> The provision of public medical and hospital services, facilities, accommodation and care (such as are not already provided for out of public funds or other private resources) for diseased or infirm poor of Dublin, and in particular those persons in need

of treatment or care by reason of illness, disease or infirmity (whether of age or otherwise). And in furtherance of and subject to the foregoing objects:

- Provision and endowment of clinical, research and training facilities and services;
- Provision and maintenance of professional, vocational, technical, paramedical and unskilled personnel required for the due operation, administration and carrying out of the said objects;
- Provision, construction and maintenance of buildings, plant and equipment and other necessary materials required for and in furtherance of the said objects.

They provided a broad scope and worthy causes which complied with them and the founders' wishes were readily identified.

The governors of Mercer's hospital had a final meeting at the Provost's House, TCD, on 3 September 1987, and the board was dissolved after 253 years. R.G. Hall was the only governor unable to attend. The first meeting of the MHF followed immediately and routine matters such as the appointment of solicitors, auditors and bankers were arranged. Registering with Revenue was next and it was decided to invite the treasurer of TCD to the next meeting to discuss management of investments. That duly happened and the governors resolved to use the treasurer, F.C. Winkelmann, and his staff as investment managers, contingent on discussions with the CCDB and their approval.[8] Dempsey, whose appointment as secretary was formally ratified at the same meeting, explored that and, all being in order, an exchange of letters between Winkelmann and the foundation occurred. In return for this service TCD was paid 0.25 per cent of the capital value of the investment at the end of each year, an arrangement that lasted until the treasurer's retirement from TCD in 1993 when he became investment manager in his own right on similar terms.[9] On 12 January 1988 arrangements with Winkelmann and TCD and a yearly payment of £750 to Dempsey for his services were formally confirmed. MHF was permitted to use the FDVH address for conduct of business. Financial affairs did not have an auspicious start and about £50,000 was lost on investment in bank shares due to a worldwide fall in stock-market values. Nonetheless, there was income of £35,377 for distribution and the first allocations were £17,500 to 'The Research Centre for Geriatric Medicine at St James's Hospital', £7,000 to 'RCSI Health Centre at the Mercer's Hospital Building' and £7,000 to 'TCD Department of Community Health and General Practice'. In consequence of MHF support all these bodies would acquire new identities in later years. The beneficiaries were informed that it was anticipated that half-yearly distributions would be made, that the annual distribution for 1988 could be three times the present distribution, depending on market conditions, that a brief statement was required of how the money was to be spent and over what period and that half-yearly reports would be required setting out how money received had been spent and funding requirements for the succeeding six months. Davis Coakley, Professor of Geriatric Medicine at TCD and St James's, had written to request permission to use the title 'Mercer's Institute for Research on Ageing (MIRA)' for the new body at St James's which was to be a major beneficiary. This was readily agreed and MIRA came into existence. Another important decision taken at the meeting was that up to 10 per cent of income would be available for distribution to other suitable charities in response to submissions. The secretary was asked to write to governors about a month ahead of the next meeting for suggestions worthy of consideration. It was reported that the CCDB had given approval for a broad range of investments.

With wind in their sails, MHF next met on 27 July 1988, an important meeting that tidied up matters from the past and set trends for the future. Legal fees totalling £25,357.35 had to be paid from the capital fund, which had a value of £1,326,224. Net disposable income was £54,022 and it was decided to distribute £40,000. This did not quite measure up to the possible triple distribution that had been suggested to the beneficiaries, but MIRA received an additional £20,000 with £8,000 each to the RCSI health centre and TCD community health and general practice. A minor allocation of £4,000 was divided between St John's House, Merrion Road, towards replacing a lift, Friends of St James's Hospital to improve general patient comfort, Northbrook House nursing home towards general running costs, and the Rotunda Hospital towards upgrading the delivery ward, setting a precedent for distributions in the succeeding years. The governors' aim was to achieve capital growth that would generate income to be distributed along similar lines. Twice-yearly meetings were planned unless exceptional circumstances arose and an audit for the sixteen months ending 31 December 1988 was arranged. On 23 February 1989 the audit was presented for approval, the capital value of the fund was £1,329,777, and donations totalling £71,500 had been made to seven recipients. Thus, with the foundation on an even keel, the governors put the years of uncertainty behind them and settled in to their new role. By 2023, forty years following the hospital closure and thirty-five from the first disbursements their support had underpinned significant progress for various recipients.

With financial support from the MHF and facilities provided by St James's Hospital, MIRA made steady progress under the direction of Coakley and his colleague J. Bernard Walsh. It was officially launched at the RCPI on 14 November 1990 with the previously mentioned performance of Boyce's anthem 'Blessed is he that considereth the sick and needy'.[10] That represented an important link to the early days and the benefit held on 12 December 1745 when the work was premiered. In 1991 MIRA was awarded a major grant by the Health Research Board (HRB) towards research into Alzheimer's disease and Ireland's first memory clinic was established. This research on ageing led to progress in clinical care and staff training and opened up new lines of investigation. Based on the results of their work, presented at national and international scientific meetings and numerous publications in peer-reviewed medical journals, they gained an international reputation and Coakley could deliver a positive account of MIRA to the governors in 1993.[11] In 1998 St James's was chosen by the DOH as the location for the National Dementia Services and Information Development Centre to lead the way and guide the delivery of dementia care in Ireland. From the outset, it was recognized that capital investment was required to provide state-of-the-art facilities for clinical care of the elderly, their rehabilitation and for teaching and research. In 1986 a draft brief was submitted to the DOH and the design team of the new St James's but economic recession was biting deeply and funds were unavailable to support this important initiative. The hospital development control plan was modified to allow for such a facility in the future, ensuring that it would be compatible with the central diagnostic and general services on campus. Inevitably the economic cycle swung in a favourable direction and in 2002 a greatly enhanced version of the 1986 proposal was submitted to the Eastern Regional Health Authority (EHRA). Around that time, Atlantic Philanthropies (AP) shifted the focus of their investment programme to the issue of ageing and care of the elderly. While the MHF continued to provide support to MIRA, major new funding came from AP, matched by the DOH, to support the appointment of a full-time professor of geriatric medicine and a senior lecturer, posts filled by Rose Anne Kenny (2005) and Joseph Harbison (2006) respectively.[12] A definitive donation of $17.1 million was then pledged by AP contingent on the balance coming from government towards the final cost of about €50 million. Despite facing the most serious financial crisis since the foundation of the state, the authorities kept faith with the project and in 2009 they committed to proceed. Construction commenced in March 2014 and the building was completed and ready for occupancy by the end of 2016. Mercer's Institute for Successful Ageing (MISA) was the first purpose-built clinical research facility for ageing on the island of Ireland. It was based on four pillars: clinical services; research excellence; training and education; and a creative life for older people. The seven-storey building has 116 in-patient beds, ambulatory care facilities, specialist areas for investigation of falls and blackouts, bone disorders, strokes, memory disorders and rehabilitation. Public spaces are designed to accommodate a range of creative activities including art exhibitions and musical performances. To complement services already on the St James's site, the day care service for older people with mental health issues was moved from St Patrick's University Hospital or Swift's Hospital as it once was. The Martha Whiteway Day Hospital was named in memory of Swift's cousin and mother-in-law to his great-nephew and early biographer, Deane Swift.[13] Thus, under MISA's roof, Mercer was linked once more with Jonathan Swift, one of her original charitable trustees. President Michael D. Higgins performed the formal opening in December 2016 and, in recognition of the fine job done, the building won an award for 'the best health building' from the Royal Institute of Architects of Ireland (RIAI) in 2017.[14] Today it fulfils its mission with distinction and the availability of such modern facilities was a major boon to patients, families and staff during the recent coronavirus (COVID) epidemic.

The general medical practice at the original hospital location has also been a resounding success under the successive leadership of Bill Shannon and Killian McGrogan. Mercer's Medical Centre (MMC) was established to serve the RCSI student population and the local community which, to a significant degree, reside in the old parishes of St Bride's, St Luke's, St Peter's and St Nicholas's without the Walls, whose sick poor were of concern to Mercer when she devised her will. After the reconstruction, the first patient was seen on 17 September 1990, over seven years after the last out-patient had attended the hospital. By then a number of allocations had been made to the RCSI by MHF and the governors were not entirely pleased that these had been used to support the building project rather than on patient care. This was strongly communicated to the RCSI's registrar, Prof. W.A.L. MacGowan, with an insistence that future allocations be spent on delivery of medical care. Perhaps this exchange accounted for the poor attendance of just four governors and the secretary when MHF met, by invitation of the RCSI, at the new health centre on 21 February 1991. Ahead of the meeting they toured the newly opened facilities and it may have been nostalgia that caused five governors to send apologies. At the meeting, Dempsey signalled that he was retiring as CEO of the FDVH and sought to retire from his position as secretary. Persuaded to remain *pro tem*, he was eventually succeeded by Richard Ensor in 1997, and he became a governor at that point.[15] He had just retired as a governor in 2006 when it was decided to buy back the portion of the old hospital building housing MMC. The deal was concluded in 2007 with an agreement that the practice would remain there with the annual rent paid back to them in return for provision of medical services to the sick poor of the area. That arrangement has served the local community well and reports are provided every six months to the governors, who keep the situation under review. MMC has received over €1.5 million of support since 1988.

Arrangements with TCD and the Department of Community Health were more complicated as the professorship of general practice and supporting structures were being developed between 1988 and 1995. The chair of Community Health existed from 1977 and Tom O'Dowd was the first professor of General Practice (est. 1991) when he took up post in 1993.[16] Over the previous five years allocations were made and set aside by MHF to support the department on foot of repeated requests from the dean of the Faculty of Health Sciences. Requested to fund the development of the chair, the governors declined and particularly rejected the suggestion that the capital be split towards this purpose. O'Dowd, by invitation, brought proposals regarding the use of the accumulated allocations to the meeting on 8 February 1994. Coincidental with his appointment, the EHRA resolved to target women's health as a major policy initiative and it was decided to recruit a practitioner with a special interest in this area with the support of the foundation. Bríd Hollywood became MHF lecturer in general practice in March 1995.[17] The Irish College of General Practitioners (ICGP) signalled their support and she joined a practice at Rossfield, Tallaght, which served a poorer area. In this context, the seal of the former hospital was adopted by MHF as the number of services using the Mercer's title increased. By 1996 €62,500 had been paid to O'Dowd and he set about developing a primary-care centre in Jobstown, Tallaght, to serve the underprivileged community there. This was built by the EHRA and in February 1999 the governors first considered a proposal to purchase the building and lease it back under an arrangement similar to that later reached with the RCSI regarding MMC. Discussions proceeded and a purchase price of £1.5 million was agreed in January 2000. By 2004, however, the plan was abandoned as final terms could not be settled and the sad legacy of the effort was a bill for legal costs of €28,258.[18] Ultimately, these fees were paid by the Health Service Executive (HSE). Undeterred, O'Dowd developed an excellent service in Jobstown and MHF continued to support the many necessary and imaginative initiatives developed under his guidance. One such was a dedicated men's health clinic, delivered by Darach Ó Ciardha. The prevalence of psychopathology among the 900 attendees in 2016 included substance abuse (alcohol or drugs) 60%, anxiety 32%, depression with suicidal ideation 24%, insomnia 24%, exposure to violence 20%, poor adult literacy 20%, sexual abuse in childhood 16%, and depression without suicidal ideation 8%. That population certainly met the definition of 'sick poor' and the governors viewed it as most worthy of support. This primary-care facility was named the HSE Mary Mercer Health Centre (MMHC) and another entity bearing the Mercer label was born. By the time COVID struck in 2020, €544,875 had been provided to support the TCD Department of

General Practice. By then, services had ceased at the MMHC, having been transferred to the newly developed Tallaght Cross Primary Care Centre in recognition of the advantages that a merger of area practices in a purpose-designed building would bring. Anti-social behaviour in Jobstown led to a break-in at MMHC during storm Emma in March 2018, ahead of its closure. In 2022 services, again supported by MHF, were restored there in response to identified need and demand. MHF support has also been provided to enhance communication between MMHC and Tallaght Cross.

In 2006 MHF began to support another medical centre in Revd James Whitelaw's old parish of St Catherine's. Thomas Court Primary Care Centre is beside St Catherine's churchyard at 1 St Catherine's Lane West. Among the services it provides is care at local facilities for homeless people, Back Lane Hostel and Sundial House, the latter a 'wet hostel' on James's Street. A harm-reduction model of care is provided there to residents with alcohol dependence. Initial support enabled the hiring of an extra practice nurse and following that funding was provided to enhance care delivered to the hostel populations. Tobacco use and alcohol and drug dependence are prevalent, leading to medical issues that include chronic obstructive pulmonary disease (COPD). With MHF support the practice developed a special programme for patients with COPD to ensure compliance with prescribed care and to support smoking cessation. Based on such initiatives, the HSE has developed specific programmes for those with chronic diseases and the foundation considers this money well spent. By 2020, Thomas Court had received €309,260 in support and that continues, most recently focused on reducing the use of benzodiazepines.

Sundial House is run by Depaul Ireland, established in Ireland in 2002 and in Northern Ireland in 2006. Depaul shares strong links with the St Vincent De Paul (SVP) charity, one of its founding partners, but is an independent organization. In 2018 they approached MHF for funding to develop a 'Homeless Health Peer Advocacy Programme (HHPA)' to support homeless people in their interactions with mainstream medical services, particularly out-patient clinic attendances. The scheme, modelled on a successful initiative in the UK, consisted of training people who had been previously homeless or substance-dependent to become peer advocates. Following induction and training, the advocates would meet and guide their clients through the hospital system. MHF agreed to a maximum one-off contribution of €80,000 in November 2018, payable in two tranches and subject to strict conditions. An initial payment of €40,000 was made in March 2019 and by the end of September the programme was underway. Nine HHPA personnel were recruited and completed induction training with the inclusion of health teams at St James's and the Mater Misericordiae hospitals and with SafetyNet, a charity aiming to see quality medical care delivered to the marginalized. With significant teething problems, particularly retention of peer advocates, and with just six hospital appointments completed, the programme continued into 2020 when it was undone by the COVID epidemic and the imposed restrictions. The second moiety of funding, due in April 2020, was not paid in the circumstances. At a meeting with MHF in early March 2020, however, Depaul indicated that funding beyond the €80,000 pledged would not be sought as the HSE Inclusion Health Programme was likely to deliver the required support. MHF had again supported an initiative deemed worthy of inclusion in mainstream services.

Many minor disbursements have been made since 1987 and these have greatly enhanced services at nursing homes, hostels and care centres. Among the agencies that have received funding is the Salvation Army, a major support to the homeless and mentally ill in Dublin. In these ways MHF continues to honour and fulfil the wishes of Mercer and her colleagues, expressed three centuries ago.

Conclusion

Male dominance in ecclesiastical, educational and political affairs meant that few women gained fame in Mercer's day. Those who did were generally figments of the imagination such as Defoe's Moll Flanders or women who lived in the shadows of prominent men, examples being Esther Johnson (Stella) and Hester Vanhomrigh (Vanessa), famous because of their association with Swift, and Mary Delany, wife of Swift's friend and fellow-cleric. Mary Wollstonecraft (1759–97), the founder of modern feminism and a woman with strong Irish associations, was but a generation later and her contemporary Maria Edgeworth (1767–1849) with an Anglo-Irish background gained fame as a novelist. This set in train a long line of famous Irish women writers. A few women have been honoured for their roles in the fight for independence such as Constance Markievicz (1868–1927), Maud Gonne (1866–1953) and Rosie Hackett (1893–1976). In 1991 the lack of recognition of women in history led to the foundation of the 'Women's Commemoration and Celebration Committee (WCCC)', which held an exhibition at the Dublin Civic Museum and in a companion volume gave an account of the ten women who featured.[1] Contextualizing the past, Margaret MacCurtain made the point that there was 'not only a need to recover information which focused on female subjects but also to look at the nature of women's work, how their reproduction affects society, their relationships of family and kinship – mothers and sons, mothers and daughters – the way work between women and men is organized socially and the manner in which women are educated. To accomplish this task is to question the political chronology, what is called the canon of history'.[2] This set a useful precedent for examining the role of women, particularly during the centenary of the momentous events in Ireland between 1914 and 1922. Despite such an academic focus, however, the most famous statue in Dublin celebrates the fictional Molly Malone, though it could be said that she represents the heroism and grit of ordinary Dublin women through the ages. Mercer and other real figures are commemorated by having streets and structures named in their honour but tourists rarely gather to be photographed beside their statues, buildings, commemorative plaques or street signs.

Looking at Mercer in the context of MacCurtain's statement, it is clear that personal wealth and contacts with prominent churchmen were her main strengths. With her family background it is likely that she received an education but she would not have had a career apart from overseeing the running of her home. As a spinster, she had no close family relationships after her parents died apart from that with her cousin Mary Barry and any other cousins there may have been. There were no descendants to honour her memory over the centuries but, despite such handicaps, her legacy has endured. It is possible, however, that the widespread 'Mercer' title may be associated by many with the clothing trade rather than her family name. It is timely, therefore, to remind people that this lady was responsible for a cascade of initiatives that commenced in 1724 and continues to flow to this day. It is remarkable how little we know of her, even when she was born, and no image exists to tell us what she looked like. Some have mistakenly chosen to represent her with a portrait of another Mary Mercer, maid to Samuel Pepys's wife Elizabeth. It is doubtful she would be flattered by that comparison and, while Pepys generally spoke kindly of the maid, he was not above subjecting her to sexual abuse and his wife to beating her when she incurred her wrath.[3] We can only wish then that her appearance reflected her generosity of heart and the goodness of her actions. It is perhaps a statement of character and lack of vanity that no portrait exists and we can judge her by her deeds rather than her looks.

The majority who leave footprints in the sands of time generally do so in a single area. Mercer is an exception in having a legacy in education, medical and nursing care and social supports such as housing. Her school, so necessary in its time to serve the needs of a vulnerable cohort, has now disappeared apart from the eponymous Mercer House at King's Hospital, but her memory remains strong in the other spheres. The residential blocks on Mercer Street have withstood the test of time and are a valuable resource when the housing stock is insufficient. Despite her limited input to the foundation of the hospital, it is in healthcare that her memory mainly survives. Though numerous health hazards have been removed or mitigated in the intervening years there are still many who live with illness, much of it associated with poverty and social disadvantage. MHF and the agencies it supports continue to care for the sick poor in line with the terms of Mercer's will and the goals of the hospital's founders. Education remains the main key to escaping the poverty trap and its consequences. In honouring the memory of this generous lady, her original plans of 1724 should not be forgotten as we reflect on the issues of homelessness, immigration and displacement that affect society today. Initiatives to address these problems can use her achievements as a motivation and an example. Finally, when a committee such as the WCCC comes to review the contribution of women to Dublin and its citizens in the future, hopefully Mary Mercer will merit due consideration.

Notes

INTRODUCTION

1 Official Dublin Street Guide: City and District (Ordnance Survey Ireland, 10th edn, 2013), p. 75.

2 J.B. Lyons, *The quality of Mercer's: the story of Mercer's Hospital, 1734–1991* (Dublin, 1991), pp 181–2.

3 Horatio Townsend, *The history of Mercer's Charitable Hospital in Dublin to the end of the year 1742* (Dublin, 1860), p. 19.

I. IN LIFE

1 Townsend, *The history of Mercer's*, p. 18.

2 Henry Cotton D.C.L., *Fasti ecclesiae Hibernicae*, ii: *the province of Leinster* (Dublin, 1848), p. 198.

3 T.P.C. Kirkpatrick, 'Mercer's Hospital: its foundation and early days', *Irish Journal of Medical Science*, 7th ser., 109 (1935), p. 2.

4 Irish Genealogy, www.irishgenealogy.ie (accessed 13 Feb. 2023).

5 Townsend, *The history of Mercer's*, p. 17.

6 *DEP*, 4–8 Mar. 1734/5.

7 C.T. M'Cready, *Dublin street names dated and explained* (Dublin, 1892, repr. 1987), p. 150.

8 www.theiveaghtrust.ie/our-story/st-brides (accessed 13 Feb. 2023).

9 Kirkpatrick, 'Mercer's Hospital', p. 3.

10 An Act (Geo. II, 25 March 1750) for Regulating the Hospital founded by Mary Mercer, Spinster (Dublin, 1817), p. 4.

11 Michael Quane, 'Mercer's School, Rathcoole and Castleknock, Co.

Dublin', *Journal of the Royal Society of Antiquaries of Ireland*, 93:1 (1963), pp 9–11 (Mercer's will is reproduced in full here).

12 An Act (Geo. II, 25 March 1750), p. 5.

13 Walter Harris, *The history and antiquities of the city of Dublin, from the earliest accounts: compiled from authentick memoirs, offices of record, manuscript collections, and other unexceptionable vouchers* (Dublin, 1766), pp 443–4.

14 Davis Coakley, *Doctor Steevens' Hospital: a brief history* (Dublin, 1992), pp 9–10.

15 L.M. Geary, *Medicine and charity in Ireland, 1718–1851* (Dublin, 2004), p. 16.

16 Jonathan Swift, 'A modest proposal for preventing the children of the poor people from being a burthen to their parents or country and for making them beneficial to the publick' in Temple Scott (ed.), *The prose works of Jonathan Swift DD*, 12 vols (London, 1925), vii, pp 203–4.

17 Victoria Glendenning, *Jonathan Swift* (London, 1999), p. 165.

18 T.E. Jordan, 'Whitelaw's "Essay on the population of Dublin": a window on late eighteenth-century housing', *New Hibernia Review/Iris Éireannach Nua*, 15:3 (2011), pp 136–45.

19 James Whitelaw, *An essay on the population of Dublin, being the result of an actual survey taken in 1798 with great care and precision, and arranged in a manner entirely new* (Dublin, 1805), p. 50.

20 K.H. Connell, 'The population of Ireland in the eighteenth century', *Economic History Review*, 16:2 (1946), pp 123–4.

21 Davis Coakley and Mary Coakley, *The history and heritage of St James's Hospital Dublin* (Dublin, 2018), pp 18–29.

22 Helen Burke, *The Royal Hospital Donnybrook: a heritage of caring, 1743–1993* (Dublin, 1993), p. 1.

23 M.V. Hanna, *The National Children's Hospital of Dublin: a social and institutional history, 1822–1998* (Dublin, 2022), p. 10.

2. IN DEATH

1 Townsend, *The history of Mercer's*, p. 28.

2 S.A.O. Fitzpatrick, *Dublin: a historical and topographical account of the city* (Dublin, 1907; repr. Cork, 1977), p. 20.

3 Diocesan & Prerogative Wills & Administrations, available at www.

nationalarchives.ie, last accessed 13 Feb. 2023.

4 Quane, *Mercer's School*, p. 16.

5 Townsend, *The history of Mercer's*, p. 21.

6 K.C. Kearns, *Dublin tenement life: an oral history* (Dublin, 1994), p. 21.

7 Quane, *Mercer's School*, p. 11.

8 Constantia Maxwell, *The stranger in Ireland from the reign of Elizabeth to the Great Famine* (Dublin, 1979; repr.), pp 137–8.

9 'Clayton, Robert', Dictionary of Irish biography, available at www.dib.ie, last accessed 13 Feb. 2023.

10 'Delany, Patrick', Dictionary of Irish biography, available at www.dib.ie, last accessed 13 Feb. 2023.

11 Angélique Day (ed.), *Letters from Georgian Ireland: the correspondence of Mary Delany, 1731–68* (Belfast, 1991), p. 10.

12 Townsend, *The history of Mercer's*, p. 26.

13 An Act (Geo. II, 25 March 1750), p. 6.

3. THE SCHOOL

1 Quane, *Mercer's School*, p. 9.

2 Ibid., p. 10.

3 NLI Ms 21 F. 52 / (079), Longfield Map Collection.

4 John D'Alton, *The history of the county of Dublin* (Dublin, 1838), pp 727–33.

5 Kerron Ó Luain, *Rathcoole and the United Irish Rebellions, 1798–1803* (Dublin, 2019), p. 12.

6 MSBM, 4 July 1743 (cited by Quane, *Mercer's School*).

7 Glendenning, *Jonathan Swift*, p. 272.

8 MSBM, 24 Feb. 1743/4.

9 Quane, *Mercer's School*, pp 18–19.

10 MSBM, 19 June 1747.

11 'Pococke, Richard', Dictionary of Irish biography, www.dib.ie (accessed 13 Feb. 2023).

12 Ó Luain, *Rathcoole and the United Irish Rebellions*, p. 15.

13 *Second report of the commissioners of Irish education inquiry* (Dublin, 1826), pp 604–7.

14 *Thirteenth report of the commissioners of the Board of Education in Ireland, 1807–12*, p. 295.

15 *First report of the commissioners on education in Ireland* (London, 1825), appendix no. 7, p. 30.

16 Ó Luain, *Rathcoole and the United Irish Rebellions*, pp 62–4.

17 Quane, *Mercer's School*, pp 26–7.

18 *Endowed Schools (Ireland) Commission,*
    1878–80 Report, I, pp 271–2.
19 *Educational Endowments (Ireland)*
    Commission: Annual Report, 1885–6,
    pp 9–10.
20 A.V. O'Connor and S.M. Parkes, *Gladly*
    learn and gladly teach: a history of Alexandra
    College and School, Dublin, 1866–1966
    (Dublin, 1966), p. 12.
21 Harris, *The history and antiquities of*
    Dublin, pp 417–18.

4. THE HOSPITAL

1   M.H. Daly, 'La Touche Bridge to
    Hoggen Green', *Dublin Historical Record,*
    7:4 (Sept.–Nov. 1945), p. 133.
2   Kirkpatrick, *Mercer's Hospital,* pp 1–2.
3   An Act (Geo. II, 25 March 1750),
    pp 4–6.
4   Harris, *The history and antiquities of*
    Dublin, p. 453.
5   An Act (Geo. II, 25 March 1750), p. 5.
6   *The picture of Dublin, for 1811; being a*
    description of the city and a correct guide
    to all the public establishments, curiosities,
    amusements, exhibitions and remarkable
    objects in and near the city of Dublin (Dublin,
    1811), pp 145–6.
7   Townsend, *The history of Mercer's,*
    pp 22–6.
8   Kirkpatrick, *Mercer's Hospital,* pp 8–9.
9   T.P. Kirkpatrick, 'Mercer's Hospital,
    Dublin', *Medical Press and Circular,* 208,
    nos 5387–8 (1942), p. 16.
10 Lyons, *The quality of Mercer's,* pp 100–1.
11 J.B. Lyons, 'Mercer's Hospital and the
    college connection', *Journal of the Irish*
    College of Physicians and Surgeons, 13:1
    (1984), pp 55–6.
12 Davis Coakley, *The Irish School of*
    Medicine: outstanding practitioners of the 19th
    century (Dublin, 1988), pp 9–16.
13 Kirkpatrick, 'Mercer's Hospital' (1942),
    pp 16–17.
14 T.P. Kirkpatrick, 'The schools of
    medicine in Dublin in the nineteenth
    century', *British Medical Journal,* 2 (1933),
    pp 110–11.
15 Lyons, *The quality of Mercer's,* pp 102–13.
16 4657367.pdf (irishgenealogy.ie), www.
    irishgenealogy.ie (accessed 13 Feb. 2023).
17 Lyons, *The quality of Mercer's,* pp 113–15.
18 *Board of Governors of Mercer's Hospital,*
    annual report for 1934 (Dublin, 1935).

19 G.M.A. Fealy, *History of apprenticeship*
    nurse training in Ireland (London, 2006),
    p. 17.
20 Cecil Woodham-Smith, *Florence*
    Nightingale, 1820–1910 (London, 1952),
    p. 256.
21 Evelyn Bolster, *The Sisters of Mercy in*
    the Crimean War (Cork, 1964), p. xix
    (introduction).
22 M.E. Doona, 'Sister Mary Joseph Croke:
    another voice from the Crimean War,
    1854–1856', *Nursing History Review,* 3
    (1995), pp 14–17.
23 Bolster, *The Sisters of Mercy,* p. xx.
24 Coakley, *Dr Steevens' Hospital,* pp 35–7.
25 Hanna, *The National Children's Hospital,*
    pp 67–8.
26 *Report on the nursing arrangements in the*
    hospitals receiving aid from the Dublin
    Hospital Sunday Fund (Dublin, 1879).
27 T.W. Grimshaw, 'Dublin Hospital
    Sunday Fund', *British Medical Journal*
    (1879), 31 May, letter to the editor,
    p. 839.
28 Lyons, *The quality of Mercer's,* p. 97.
29 *Dublin Hospitals Commission: report of*
    inquiry, 1887, together with minutes of
    evidence and appendices (Dublin, 1887).
30 Ibid., p. 69 (response to queries 1645 and
    1646).
31 Fealy, *History of apprenticeship nurse*
    training, p. 43.
32 *Dublin Hospitals Commission: report of*
    inquiry, 1887, p. xxxix, clauses 299–301.
33 NAI PRIV 1269/1/1, *Minute Book of the*
    Board of Governors of Mercer's Hospital, 9
    Feb. 1898.
34 Fealy, *History of apprenticeship nurse*
    training, p. 48.
35 Lyons, *The quality of Mercer's,* pp 121–3.
36 Fealy, *History of apprenticeship nurse*
    training, pp 59–60.
37 *Dublin Hospitals Commission: report of*
    inquiry, 1887, appendix Q.
38 5620552.pdf (irishgenealogy.ie), www.
    irishgenealogy.ie (accessed 13 Feb. 2023).
39 NAI PRIV 1269/1/31, *Minute Book of the*
    Medical Board of Mercer's Hospital, 8 July
    1912.
40 *Board of Governors of Mercer's Hospital,*
    annual report for 1916 (Dublin, 1917).
41 4201061.pdf (irishgenealogy.ie), www.
    irishgenealogy.ie (accessed 13 Feb. 2023).

5. FUNDING THROUGH ORATORIO, ORATIONS AND ODDS

1 Triona O'Hanlon, 'Music for Mercer's: the Mercer's Hospital music collection and charity music in eighteenth-century Dublin' (PhD, Technological University Dublin, 2012), pp 17–20.

2 Harris, *The history and antiquities of Dublin*, pp 452–3.

3 NAI PRIV 1269/1/1, 28 May 1736.

4 Townsend, *The history of Mercer's*, p. 40.

5 'Dubourg, Matthew', *Dictionary of Irish biography*, www.dib.ie (accessed 13 Feb. 2023).

6 Burke, *The Royal Hospital Donnybrook*, p. 9.

7 Townsend, *The history of Mercer's*, appendix II, pp 44–54.

8 'McGuckin, (Bartholomew) Barton', *Dictionary of Irish biography*, www.dib.ie (accessed 13 Feb. 2023).

9 *Dublin Hospitals Commission: Report of Inquiry, 1887*, p. 74.

10 O'Hanlon, *Music for Mercer's*, p. 71.

11 *PO*, 6–10 Apr. 1736.

12 Geary, *Medicine and charity*, p. 3.

13 Tony Farmar, *Patients, potions and physicians: a social history of medicine in Ireland* (Dublin, 2004), p. 49.

14 Constantia Maxwell, *Dublin under the Georges* (Dublin, 1997; repr.), p. 171.

15 J. Warburton, J. Whitelaw and Robert Walsh, *History of the city of Dublin, from the earliest accounts to the present time, containing its annals, antiquities, ecclesiastical history and charters; its present extent, public buildings, schools, institutions etc.; to which are added biographical notices of eminent men and copious appendices of its population, revenue, commerce and literature* (2 vols, London, 1818), ii, pp 868–9.

16 NAI/CSO/RP/1831/2653/1.

17 NAI/CSO/RP/1831/2653/2.

18 PO, 30 Jan.–3 Feb. 1742.

19 NAI PRIV 1269/1/1, 21 Nov. 1741.

20 Ibid., 12 Dec. 1741, 2 Jan. 1742.

21 Donald Burrows and Rosemary Dunhill (eds), *Music and theatre in Handel's world: the family papers of James Harris, 1732–1780* (New York, 2002), p. 131, letter dated 10 Dec. 1741, 4th earl of Shaftsbury to James Harris [Salisbury], Hants Record Office, 9M73/G350/22/1.

22 Lyons, *The quality of Mercer's*, p. 182.

23 Horatio Townsend, *An account of the visit of Handel to Dublin, with notices of his life and character* (Dublin, 1861), p. 36.

24 *FJ*, 26–9 Dec. 1741.

25 *FJ*, 3–6 Apr. 1742.

26 Townsend, *The visit of Handel to Dublin*, pp 49–52.

27 *FJ*, 13–17 Apr. 1742.

28 NAI PRIV 1269/1/1, 4 Mar. 1742.

29 *FJ*, 13–17 Apr. 1742.

30 *FJ*, 10–14 Jan. 1743–4.

31 Lyons, *The quality of Mercer's*, p. 36.

32 Ibid., pp 78–9.

33 Kirkpatrick, *Mercer's Hospital*, p. 6.

34 Geary, *Medicine and charity*, pp 35–6.

35 Samuel Croker-King, *A short history of the hospital founded by Doctor Richard Steevens, near the city of Dublin, from its establishment in the year 1717 to the present time, 1785* (Dublin, 1854), pp 30–3.

6. THE STREET AND BUILDINGS

1 Townsend, *The history of Mercer's*, p. 21.

2 McCready, *Dublin street names*, p. 66.

3 Clive Lee (ed.), *Surgeons Halls: building the Royal College of Surgeons in Ireland, 1810–2010* (Dublin, 2011), p. 16.

4 McCready, *Dublin street names*, p. 39.

5 Kirkpatrick, *Mercer's Hospital*, pp 12–13.

6 Lyons, *Mercer's Hospital*, pp 54–5.

7 Ibid., p. 53.

8 Kirkpatrick, *Mercer's Hospital*, p. 12.

9 C.A. Cameron, *Report upon the state of public health and the sanitary work performed in Dublin during the year 1903* (Dublin, 1904), p. 106.

10 'O'Rourke, Horace Tennyson', *Dictionary of Irish biography*, www.dib.ie (accessed 13 Feb. 2023).

11 'Simms, Herbert George', *Dictionary of Irish biography*, www.dib.ie (accessed 13 Feb. 2023).

12 Ruth McManus, *Dublin, 1910–1940: shaping the city and suburbs* (Dublin, 2002).

13 Brian Behan, *Mother of all the Behans: the autobiography of Kathleen Behan as told to Brian Behan* (London, 1984), pp 87–99.

14 4202975.pdf (irishgenealogy.ie), www.irishgenealogy.ie (accessed 13 Feb. 2023).

7. MERCER'S HOSPITAL FOUNDATION

1 Lyons, *The quality of Mercer's*, pp 181–2.

2   William Watts, *Provost, Trinity College Dublin: a memoir* (Dublin, 2008), p. 162.
3   MHB minutes, 25 Feb. 1985.
4   David Fitzpatrick (ed.), *The Feds: an account of the Federated Dublin Voluntary Hospitals, 1961–2005* (Dublin, 2006), p. 14.
5   Ibid., p. 275.
6   MHB minutes, 25 Nov. 1985.
7   MHF minutes, 3 Sept. 1987.
8   MHF minutes, 29 Sept. 1987.
9   MHF minutes, 27 July 1993.
10 Lyons, *The quality of Mercers*, p. 182.
11 MHF minutes, 3 Feb. 1993.
12 Coakley and Coakley, *The history and heritage of St James's Hospital*, p. 396.
13 Glendenning, *Jonathan Swift*, p. 1.

14 Coakley and Coakley, *St James's Hospital*, p. 398.
15 MHF minutes, 26 Feb. 1997.
16 MHF minutes, 27 July 1993.
17 MHF minutes, 25 July 1995.
18 MHF minutes, 25 Feb. 2004.

CONCLUSION

1   Women's Commemoration and Celebration Committee, *Ten Dublin women* (Dublin, 1991).
2   Margaret MacCurtain, 'The "ordinary" heroine: women into history' in Women's Commemoration and Celebration Committee, *Ten Dublin women* (Dublin, 1991), p. 7.
3   Lord Braybrooke (ed.), *The diary of Samuel Pepys esquire* (London, nd), p. 455.

Index